IRELAND'S ANCIENT EAST

CARSTEN KRIEGER

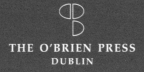

THE O'BRIEN PRESS
DUBLIN

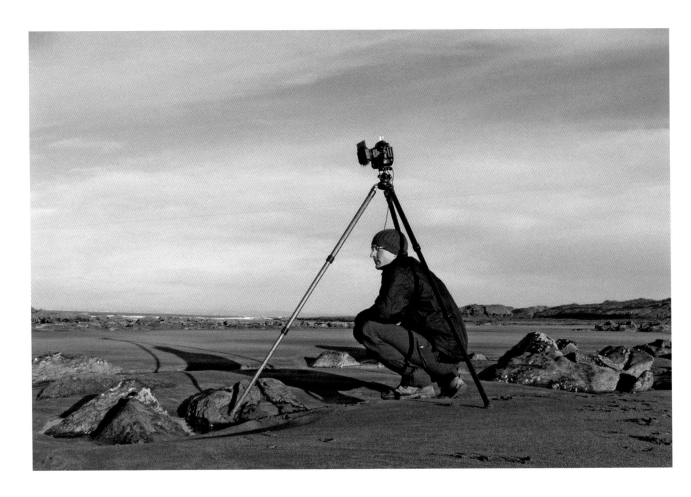

CARSTEN KRIEGER is a professional photographer based in the west of Ireland. His unique images are highly acclaimed and over the past decade he has become one of Ireland's foremost photographers covering various topics from landscape and nature to architecture and food photography.

He has published numerous books on Ireland's landscape, wildlife and heritage including the popular *Ireland's Wild Atlantic Way* and regularly works for Fáilte Ireland, The UNESCO Burren and Cliffs of Moher Geopark and other clients.

This book wouldn't have been possible without the people and organisations who put a lot of time, effort and money into keeping Ireland's historic sites alive and who opened their doors for me.

A big thank you to the people at the following sites who all went out of their way to accommodate me and made each shoot a special experience: Uisneach, Birr Castle, The National Stud, Charleville Castle, Jerpoint Glass, Blackwater Castle, Lismore Castle, Rothe House, Waterford Treasures, Enniscorthy Castle, Powerscourt Estate, Russborough House and the Wicklow Gaol.

A big thank you also goes to the Office of Public Works and the helpful staff at the various OPW sites.

CONTENTS

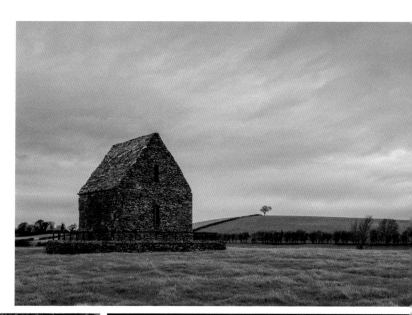

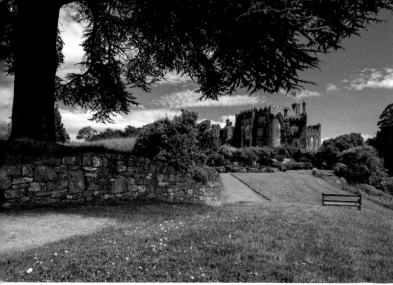

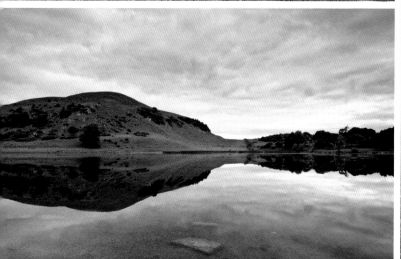

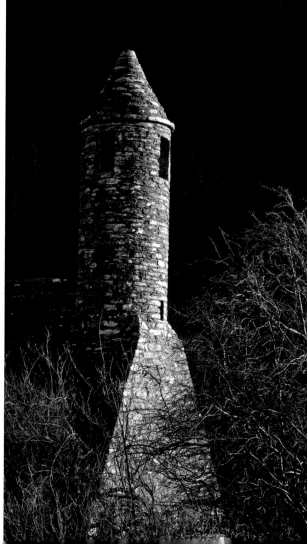

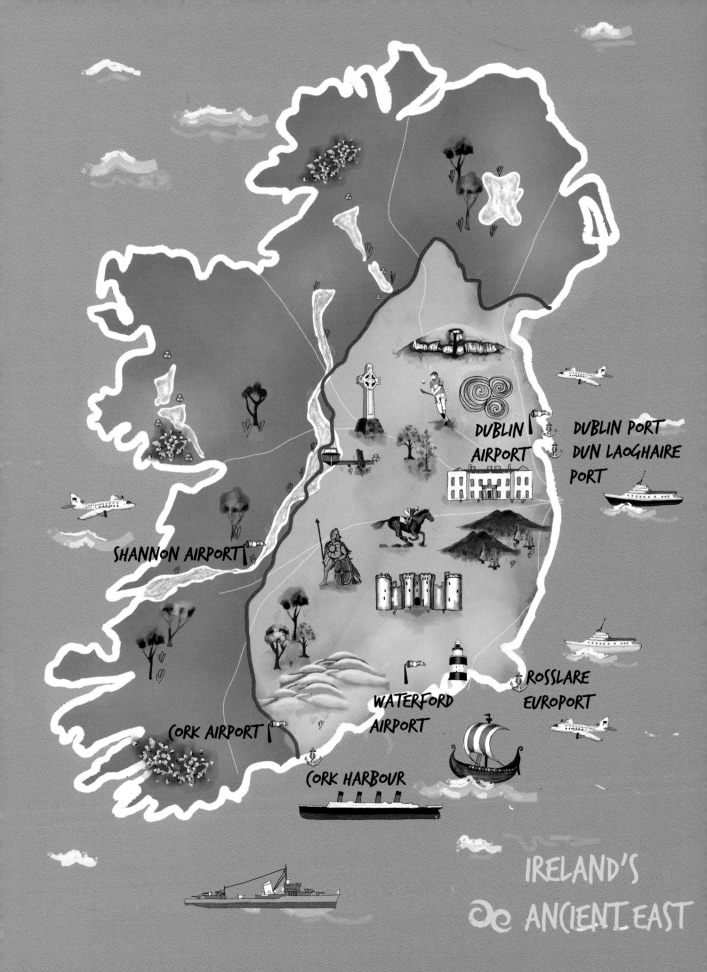

DUBLIN
AIRPORT

DUBLIN PORT
DUN LAOGHAIRE
PORT

SHANNON AIRPORT

ROSSLARE
EUROPORT

WATERFORD
AIRPORT

CORK AIRPORT

CORK HARBOUR

IRELAND'S
ANCIENT EAST

INTRODUCTION

There are few countries where history is such an obvious part of daily life as it is in Ireland. There hardly is a road or path that doesn't lead past an old church, the ruin of a castle or the remains of an ancient homestead. In places the landscape is like a living history book, and with a little bit of imagination it is easy to relive Ireland's past. After the success of the *Wild Atlantic Way*, a 2,500-kilometre touring route along Ireland's west coast, the Irish Tourist Board created *Ireland's Ancient East* to highlight and celebrate Ireland's history and heritage. For me this meant packing up my gear and going on another road trip. But while travelling the *Wild Atlantic Way* is very straightforward, just follow the route and take in the scenery, visiting the *Ancient East* is more of an expedition, a journey into a land of stories.

Ireland has a long tradition of storytelling. The *seanchaí*, traditional storytellers, were once high-ranking members of the clans with the task to preserve historic events and pass it on from generation to generation. Later, after the downfall of the clan system, the *seanchaí* would travel around the country, from place to place sharing their stories. In those times, before radio and television, they would be invited into someone's home where often the whole neighbourhood would gather to listen to tales

of adventure and magic. These tales tell the history of Ireland from the earliest days. More often than not fiction mingles with fact, but it is hard to tell where one ends and the other starts. It's these stories and their connection to the actual places and buildings you can visit that makes Irish history, and Ireland's Ancient East so interesting: Mysterious druids, mighty warriors, chieftains and kings, saints and monks, they all left their legacy and stay alive through it; travelling the *Ancient East* means following these stories like a trail of breadcrumbs.

The official Ireland's Ancient East website features nine Irish stories and their effects on the built and natural landscape: Ancient Ireland, Big Houses and Hard Times, Castles and Conquests, Maritime Gateway, High Kings and Heroes, Sacred Ireland, Vikings, The Sport of Kings and Ireland's Mystical Waterway. They feature throughout the book and are excellent places to start – the first breadcrumb, so to speak – in planning your journey. They are all interconnected, so you will find yourself moving from the Sacred Ireland to Ireland's Mystical Waterway, from Vikings to Castles and Conquests and so on; it doesn't really matter where you start: Newgrange, Clonmacnoise or the Rock of Cashel to name but a few. While wandering around exploring you will come across

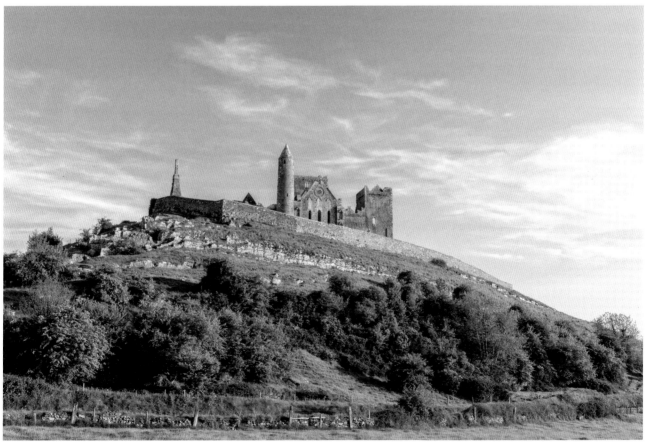

Rock of Cashel, Co. Tipperary

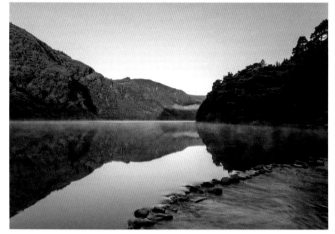

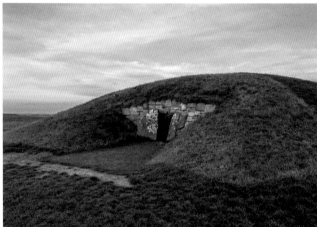

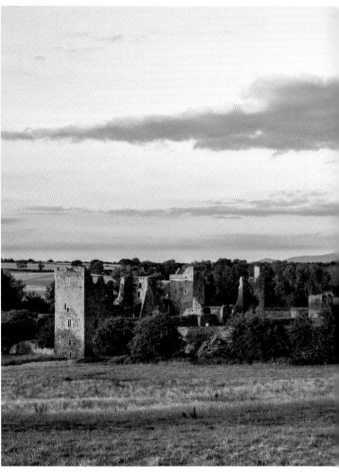

stories and legends that will mesmerise you. But because the stories and legends never really end they will lead you to other places not too far away and so you travel on. And so it goes, from story to story, from place to place, breadcrumb to breadcrumb, all around *Ireland's Ancient East* from County Louth in the north east to County Cork in the south.

For this book I found my own trail of breadcrumbs, picking up a new story where the last one left off. But as with every book there is unfortunately only so much space and many places fell victim to the lack of time and the editing process. Fourknocks in Co. Meath was one of those, a passage tomb with an unusual, large central chamber; Clonard also in Co. Meath was the site of one of the oldest monastic settlements in Ireland; Fethard, a small town in Co. Tipperary, features a number of medieval

ruins including town walls and gates, a friary and fortified town houses; or the Cavan Burren, a limestone plateau with an impressive collection of Neolithic tombs. The list goes on and on. Although this book is finished my own journey won't be for quite a while and I will return to the *Ancient East* for the foreseeable future. There is so much more to see and learn, enough to fill a few more books.

This book isn't meant as a guide book, even less as a history book, but it hopefully will give you a clue on where to start your own journey and the wealth of story and legend out there. Now go and find your breadcrumbs.

Carsten Krieger,

Spring 2017

Left page top: Upper Lake, Glendalough, Co. Wicklow
Left page bottom: Hill of Tara, Co. Meath
Centre: Kells Priory, Co. Kilkenny
Right page top: Charleville Castle, Co Cork
Right page bottom: St Brigid's Cathedral, Co. Kildare

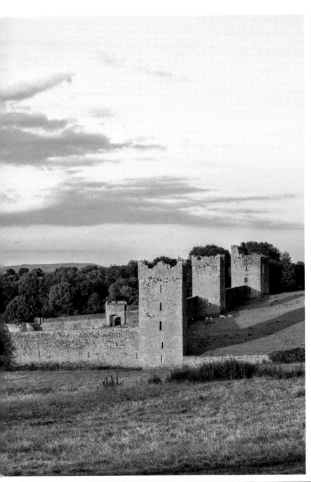

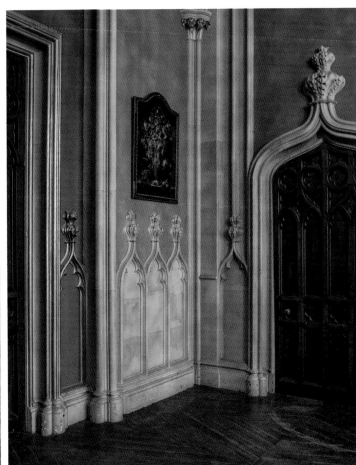

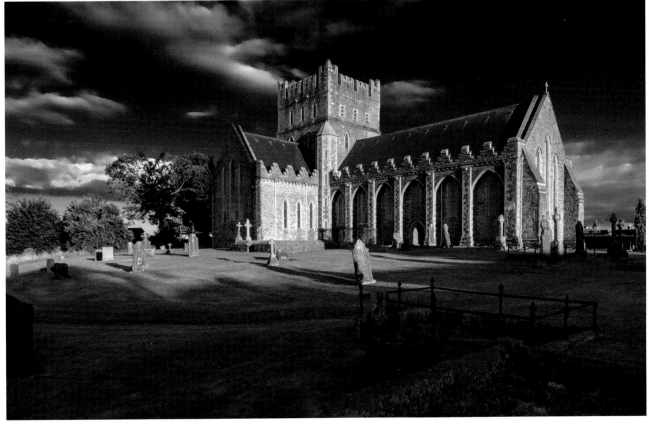

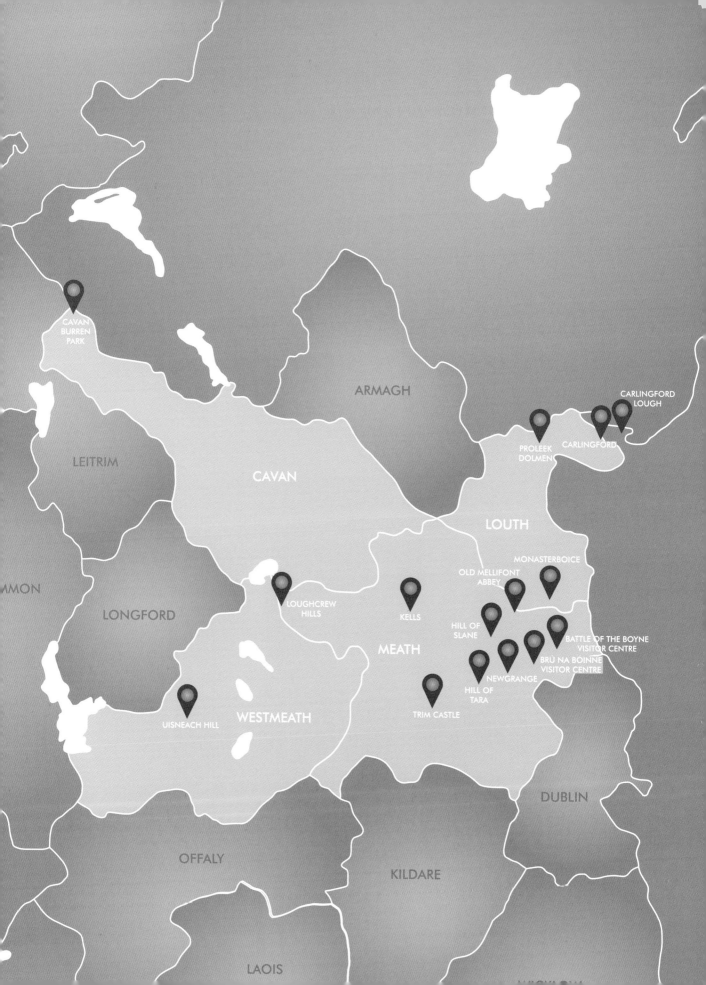

THE CRADLE OF CIVILISATION

I've seen Eire's beautiful castles
And its history, I've learned so well
I've read of the High Kings of Tara
And the wonderful Book of Kells
Where on Slane, they remember St. Patrick
He lit fire for the people to see
'Ere he brought love and kindness to Ireland
And the beautiful County of Meath

Nelson/Copyright Green Grass Music

The River Boyne rises near the Hill of Carbury in County Kildare and enters the Irish Sea near Drogheda in County Louth. For most of its course, however, it runs through County Meath and so the Boyne is very much Meath's river.

In its upper reaches the Boyne is a river like many others, but several miles downstream, when it reaches the town of Trim, the unprepossessing river, with the support of several tributaries, has grown into the mighty torrent that attracted settlers since the earliest times and inspired poets and other artists including William Wilde, father of the more famous Oscar.

It possesses charms and beauties ... without a rival in this or perhaps any other country. Slow, calm, and tranquil in its early course, the mower whets his scythe in the deep meadows by its brink, and the reaper gathers the corn from the very margin of its waters; the swift and the martin skim over its clear surface, and the robin sings in the ancient thorn that rises out of the adjoining hedgerow. The very mayfly, as it lights upon it, breaks the mirror of its surface. The wide-spreading circles which mark the springing of the trout, or the timid breathing of the roach, are all, save the flapping of the water-hen, or the easy paddle of the baldcoot, that disturb its placid bosom.

William Wilde, *The Beauties of the Boyne and its tributary the Blackwater*, 1849

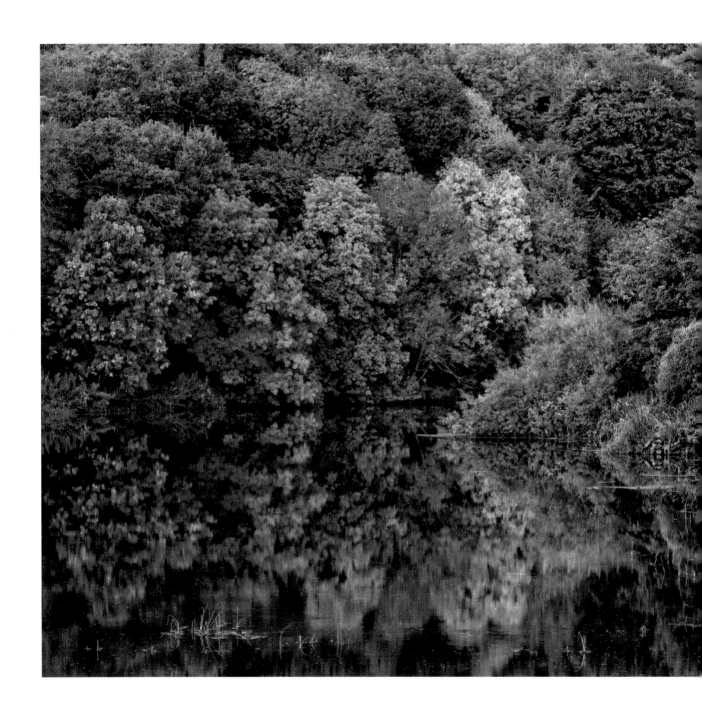

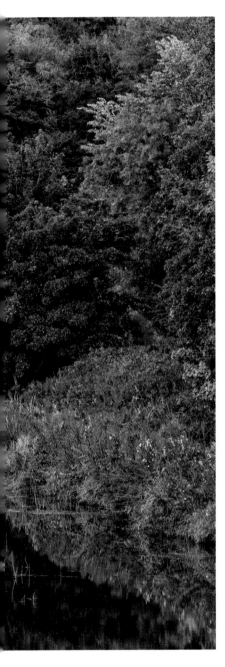

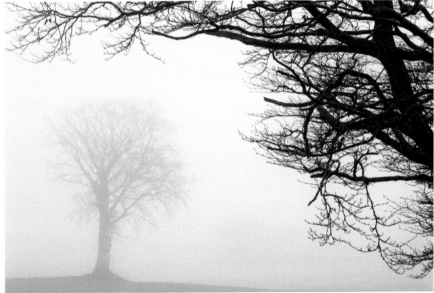

Left: The River Boyne near Navan, Co. Meath
Above: Trees and Fog, Co. Meath

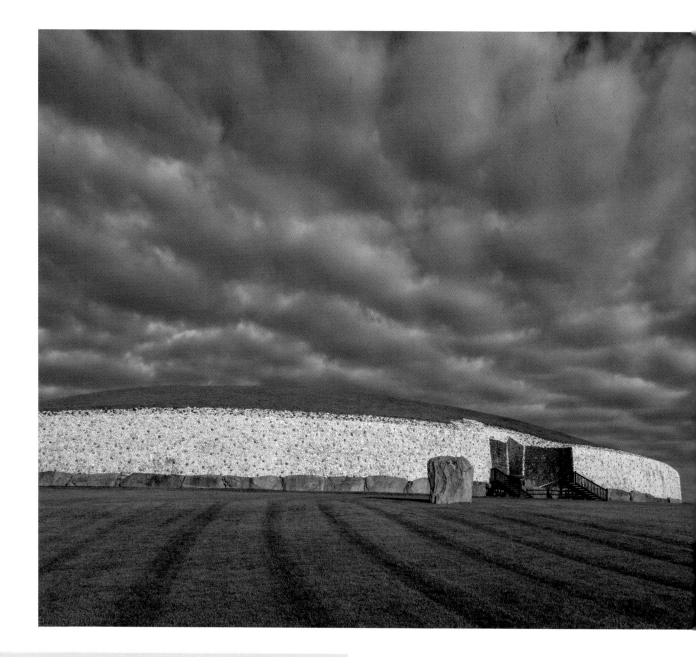

ANCIENT IRELAND

The Boyne Valley must have been a very attractive location for the new Stone Age settlers. The River Boyne provided drinking water and food in the form of salmon and other fish and its floodplain would have been ideal for cultivating and grazing. The hills surrounding the river valley were rich in woodlands of oak and birch and the Antrim coast, only a few days travel away, provided deposits of flintstones to make knives, arrow heads and other tools.

The lasting achievement of the Boyne Valley people is Newgrange, a passage tomb built on a long hill overlooking the bending and looping river and its valley. Before Newgrange an earthen mound stood here, which shows that this particular place must have already had significance. The most striking feature of Newgrange is its association with the winter solstice, the shortest day of the year. Around 21 December the rising sun illuminates the passage and inner chamber where the remains of the ancestors would have rested. The winter solstice meant the rebirth of the sun after the dark winter days. From this day onward, days would be longer and winter would come to an end. Another theory suggests that the rays of the sun would also rejuvenate the spirits of the ancestors and create a link between the world of the living and the dead.

The construction of Newgrange must have taken many years: the builders needed to carefully calculate the location and orientation of the building to ensure the rising sun on the winter solstice would illuminate the inner chamber and they would have needed to move stones of various sizes and weights for miles to the building site. About 450 large slab stones measuring up to four metres in length and weighing over a tonne each formed the core of the passage tomb.

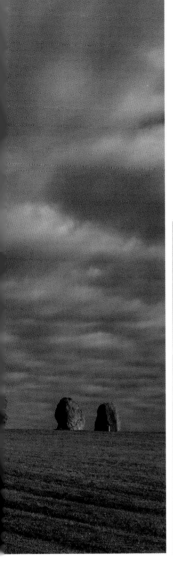

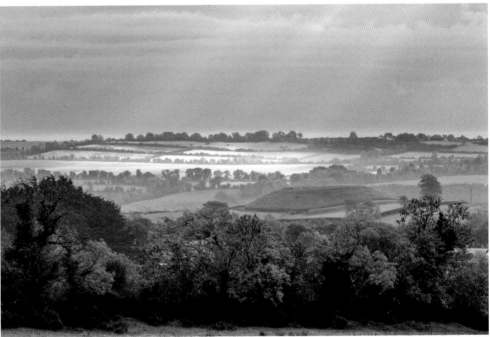

Left page: Newgrange, Co. Meath
Right page: Newgrange seen from Knowth, Co. Meath

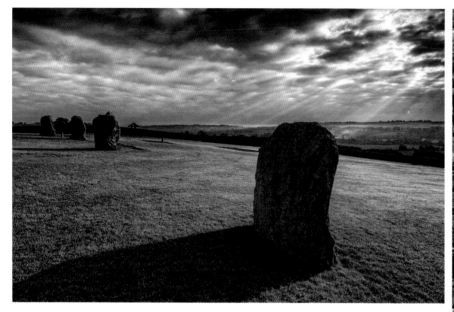

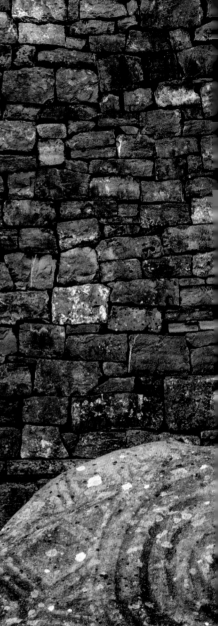

For the mound some 200,000 tonnes of hand-sized pebbles from the Boyne riverbed were used and stones of quartz and granite made an imposing white facade. The quartz came from County Wicklow, around 80km to the south, and the granite originated at Dundalk Bay, 50km to the north. When finished, Newgrange was some twelve metres high and measured 80 metres across. Its bright white facade is visible for miles around in all kinds of weather and dominates the landscape of the Boyne Valley.

Close by stand two more imposing passage tombs. Dowth derives its name from the Irish *Sí Dubhaidh*, The Fairy Mound of Darkness. Legend tells us that the mound was built by King Bressal Bodibad who had set his mind on building a mound that would reach up to the heavens. To achieve his goal he persuaded his sister, a sorceress, to stop the sun in the sky so the day would never end. He then put all the men in Ireland to work. Unfortunately at some time during this long day he offended his sister who immediately lifted her spell. Darkness descended and all the workers left. From this day on the place was known as the Fairy Mound of Darkness.

Unlike most passage tombs, Dowth has two passages and chambers both located at the western side of the mound. The one known as southern passage and chamber is aligned to catch the light at sunset on the winter solstice day. During excavations quartz debris was found, which suggests that Dowth once had the same finish as Newgrange.

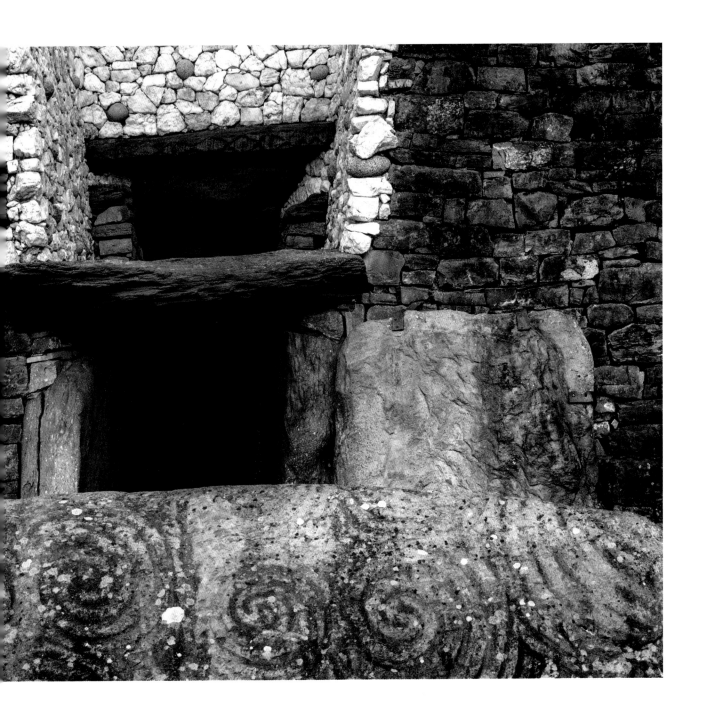

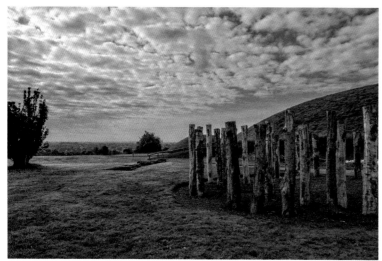

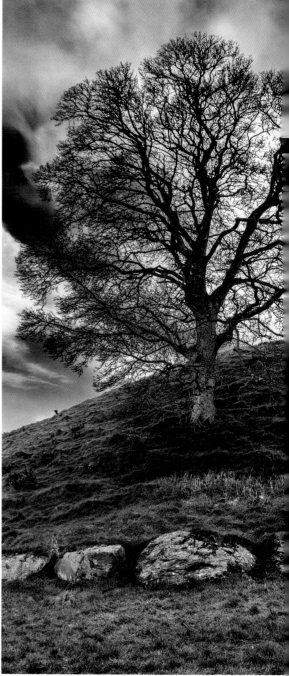

Knowth is the most complicated and mysterious of the Boyne Valley passage tombs; its complex consists of a massive central mound surrounded by eighteen smaller satellite tombs. The main mound covers two passages – only discovered in 1967 and 1968 – one facing west, the other east. Unlike Newgrange and Dowth, Knowth is aligned to catch sunrise (eastern passage and chamber) and sunset (western passage and chamber) at the equinoxes on 21 March and 21 September.

The passage tombs of the Boyne Valley, created by Neolithic people, stood the test of time and remained in use for thousands of years, not always as intended – the rather eccentric Lord Netterville erected a small tea house on top of the Dowth sometime in the eighteenth century.

Knowth was being used as a settlement and burial place until the early Bronze Age (c. 2000 BC) before being abandoned. Around 300 AD a Celtic tribe took over, transforming it into a fortified dwelling. Over the following centuries Knowth survived battles, Viking raids, became capital of the Celtic kingdom of North Brega, was given to the Cistercian Abbey at Mellifont, converted into a Norman motte and eventually used as a farm. This last was the destiny of all three sites before they were purchased and placed under protection by the Irish State.

Left page top: Knowth, Co. Meath
Left page: The tree at Dowth, Co. Meath
Right page: Entrance Passage, Knowth Main Tomb, Co. Meath

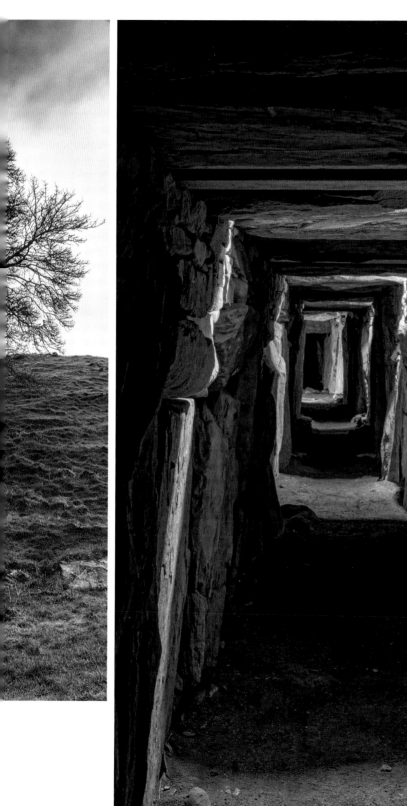
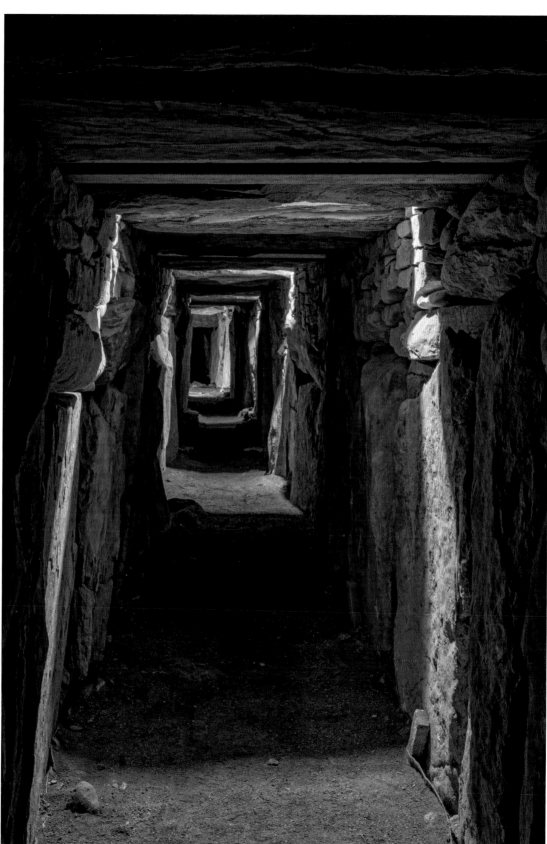

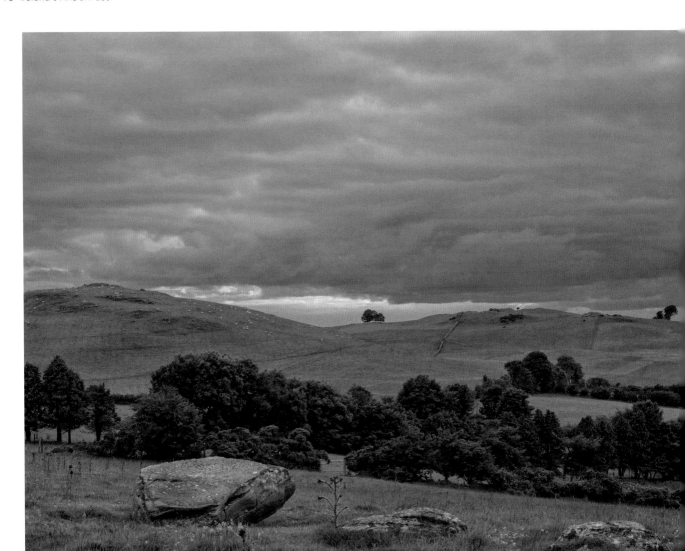

Determined now her tomb to build,
Her ample skirt with stones she filled,
And dropped a heap on Carnmore;
Then stepped one thousand yards, to Loar,
And dropped another goodly heap;
And then with one prodigious leap Gained Carnbeg;
and on its height Displayed the wonders of her might.
And when approached death's awful doom,
Her chair was placed within the womb
Of hills whose tops with heather bloom

Jonathan Swift, c. 1720

The hills of Loughcrew or *Sliabh na Caillighe* (The Hill of the Witch) form a chain of to the north west of the Boyne Valley that rises to overlook the plains of County Meath and County Cavan. On top of these hills can be found one of the greatest collections of megalithic passage tombs in Ireland, dating back more than 5,000 years.

Legend has it that the cairns were left there by Garavogue, a giant witch, who performed a ritual to give her the power to rule all of Ireland. The task was to hop from one hill to the next while keeping a load of stones in her apron. Another version of the story tells us she had to drop a certain number of stones from her apron on each hilltop while remaining airborne. Both versions however have the same outcome in that the witch miscalculated her last leap and fell to her death.

Passage tombs are the most advanced form of megalithic tombs and consist of a distinctive passage leading into a central chamber, either

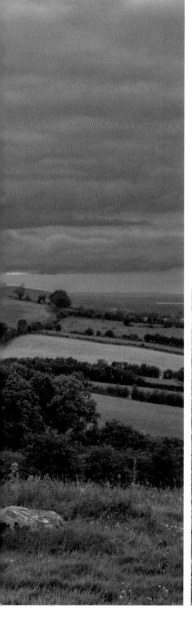

Left page: The Loughcrew Hills, Co. Meath
Right page: Entrance Passage of Cairn T, Carnbane East, Loughcrew, Co. Meath

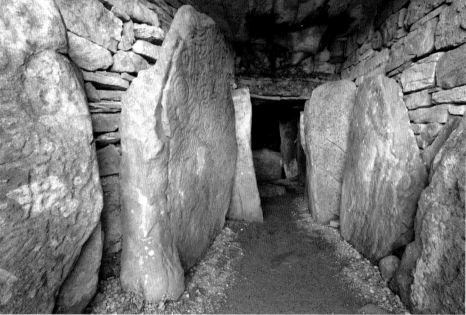

cruciform, rectangular or polygonal. This structure is covered by a mound of rough stones, a cairn, which is often bordered by upright kerb stones. The kerb stones that also form the passage and chamber are often decorated with incised motives known as 'megalithic art'.

Although these passage tombs have been used as burial places, and cremated human bones and artefacts like pottery, pins, bones and pendants have been found inside, they also have an important spiritual component.

Passage tombs are frequently located on high ground, the meeting place of earth – where people dwell – and sky, the seat of the gods. At Loughcrew more than thirty passage tombs of various sizes are placed on or close to the top of the three hills at Carnbane East, Carnbane West and Patrickstown.

As in many passage tombs, the entrance passages at Loughcrew are aligned to catch the sun; Loughcrew Cairn T (on Carnbane East)

catches the sun at the equinoxes (when night and day are of equal length), Cairn L (on Carnbane West) does so at the ancient festivals of Samhain (marking the start of winter, nowadays better known as Halloween) and Imbolc (marking the start of spring, nowadays St Brigid's Day). On these days the sun illuminates the megalithic art on the main kerbstone. One theory is that the carvings in the kerb stones represent the movements of celestial bodies like the sun or moon in the sky in conjunction with the monuments on the ground.

The Loughcrew group of passage tombs is also aligned in an east to west direction with the number of monuments increasing with each peak. Another interesting fact is that at least six of the cairns at Loughcrew point towards the passage tomb of Fourknocks some fifty kilometres to the south east.

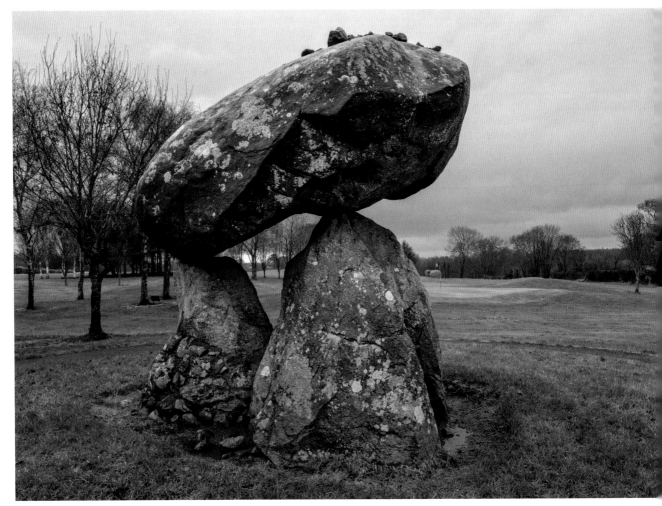

The Proleek Portal Tomb stands in a rather unlikely location these days: at the edge of a golf course! It dates from around 3,000BC and its capstone is estimated to weigh around 40 tonnes. It is not surprising that this structure is at the centre of many legends. According to one, a Scottish giant, Parrah Boug MacShagean, has carried the capstone to its current location when he was in the area to fight the local giant Fin MacCool (Fionn Mac Cumhaill).

They say it is the grave of Para Buidhe Mór Mhac Seoidín, a Scotch giant, who came to challenge Fin Mac Coole … Para Buidhe Mór asked Fin's wife where he (Fin) used to eat, Fin, she told him, when he was hungry would kill one of those bullocks (pointing to them), roast him and eat him. Para went and did the same; the spot on which he killed, roasted, and ate the bullock, is pointed out yet …When he had eaten he went to the river which runs near the spot, to satisfy his thirst; but Fin threw poison into the river, by which means he dispatched him (Co. Louth Ordnance Survey Letters, 1836).

Another legend says that if you throw a pebble onto the capstone and it stays there you will be married within the year. Another version promises you a wish if you manage to throw three stones on top.

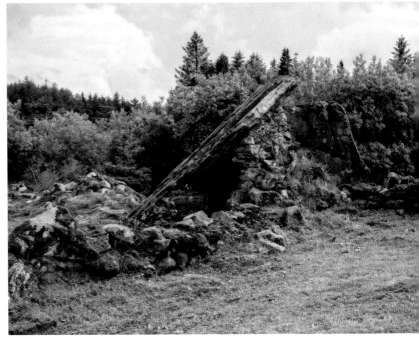

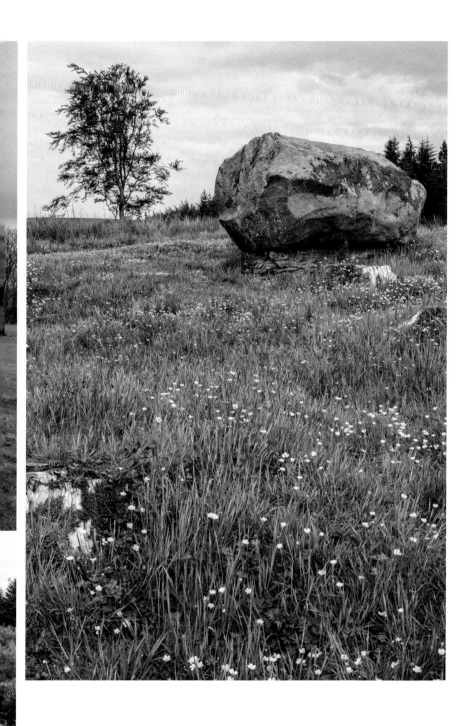

Left page top: Proleek Portal Tomb, Co. Louth
Left page bottom: Calf House Portal Tomb, The Cavan Burren
Right page: The Cavan Burren is a small area of limestone karst and has been named after
its big brother in Co. Clare. The area hosts a dense accumulation of neolithic structures
and is thought to have been inhabited since 4500BC. The Cavan Burren is now part of the
Marble Arch Caves Global Geopark.

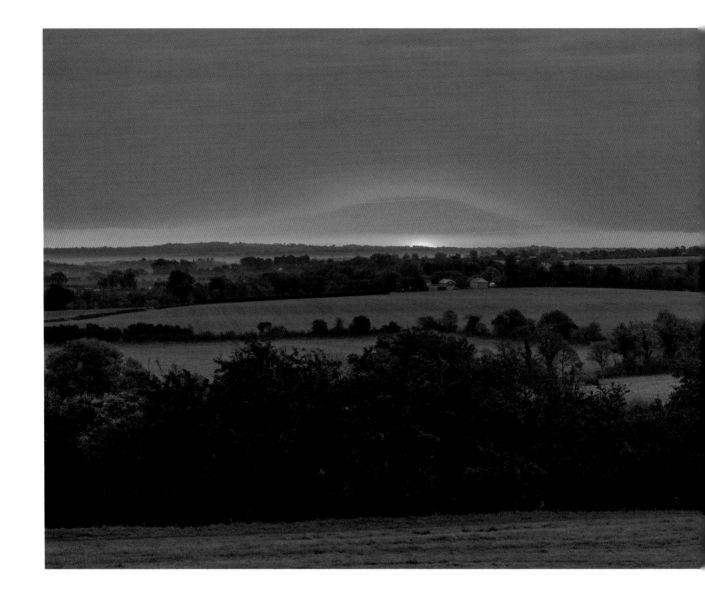

HIGH KINGS AND HEROES

The Hill of Tara is a moderate elevation near the town of Navan, County Meath overlooking the Boyne and Blackwater Valleys below. Its name derives from the Irish *Teamhair*, *Place of great prospect* or *Place with a wide view*. Today it isn't much more than a grassy pasture with bumps and hollows, but it is one of the oldest and most important historic sites in Ireland.

The Hill of Tara is best known as the coronation place of the early Irish kings and some 142 kings are said to have started their reign here. The story of Tara, however, starts well before it became a coronation site.

The oldest structure on the Hill of Tara is the *Mound of Hostages* (*Duma na nGiall*), a passage tomb that dates back to around 2500 BC and which contained the cremated remains of at least 200 individuals and the skeleton of a fourteen-year-old boy decorated with a necklace with beads of bronze, amber, jet and faience.

Later the tomb was used by the Celtic kings, like Niall of the Nine

hostages, to hold adversaries; he is said to have held hostages from every province in Ireland and Britain to ensure their submission to his rule.

Close to the Mound of Hostages are the King's Seat (*Forradh*) with the Stone of Destiny (*Lia Fáil*) and Cormac's House (*Teach Chormaic*).

The King's Seat was most likely the inauguration site for the kings of old. The current mound dates from the early centuries AD, was built on top of older mounds and could have featured a circular house. In the legends the site is also the burial place of the Spanish princess, Tea. Her wish was to be buried under the fairest hill in Ireland and her husband chose Tara.

The Stone of Destiny was moved to its current location in 1798 after the Battle of Tara to mark the graves of some four hundred United Irishmen who fell during the fight. Originally it stood just north of the Mound of Hostages where it was placed by the Tuatha DeDannann tribe (the people of the goddess Danu) as one of their sacred objects. Legend tells us that the stone would roar out once the rightful king touched it.

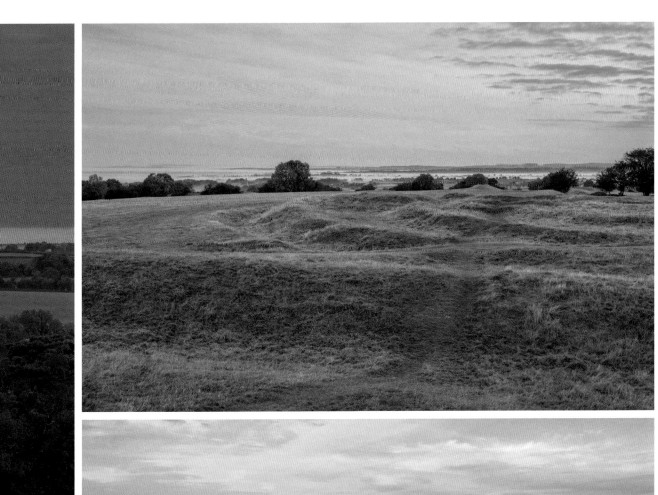

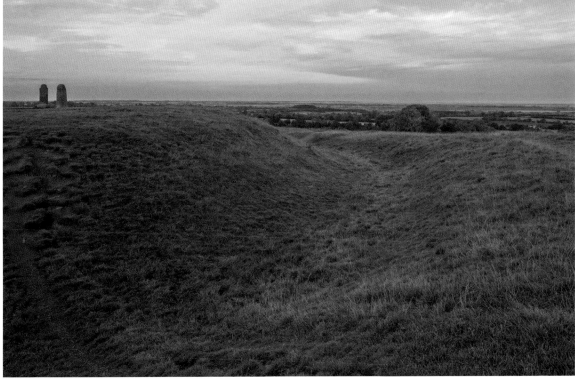

Left page: Sunrise, Hill of Tara, Co. Meath
Right page top: Rath of the Synods, Hill of Tara, Co. Meath
Right page bottom: Rath of the Kings, Hill of Tara, Co. Meath

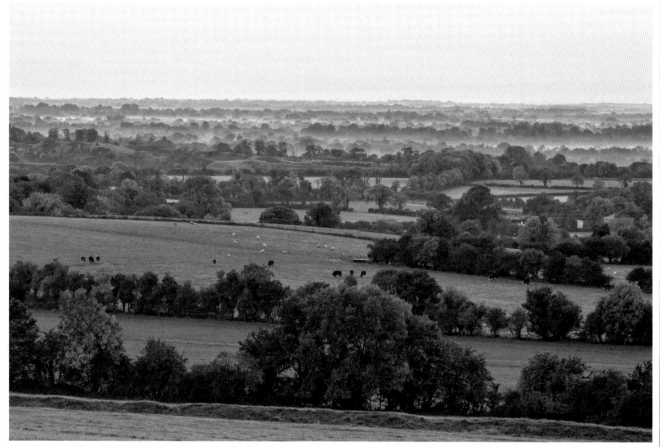

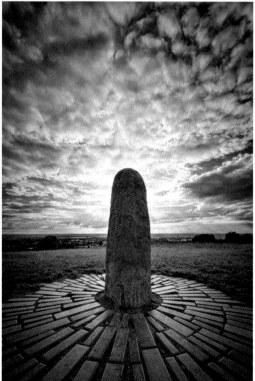

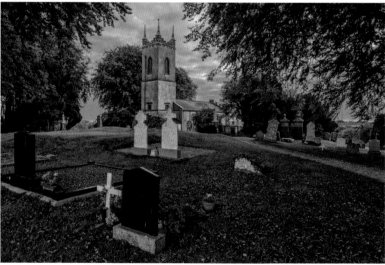

Left page top: View from the Hill of Tara, Co. Meath
Left page bottom left: Stone of Destiny, Hill of Tara, Co. Meath
Left page bottom right: St Patrick's Church, Hill of Tara, Co. Meath
Right page: Rag Trees, Hill of Tara, Co. Meath

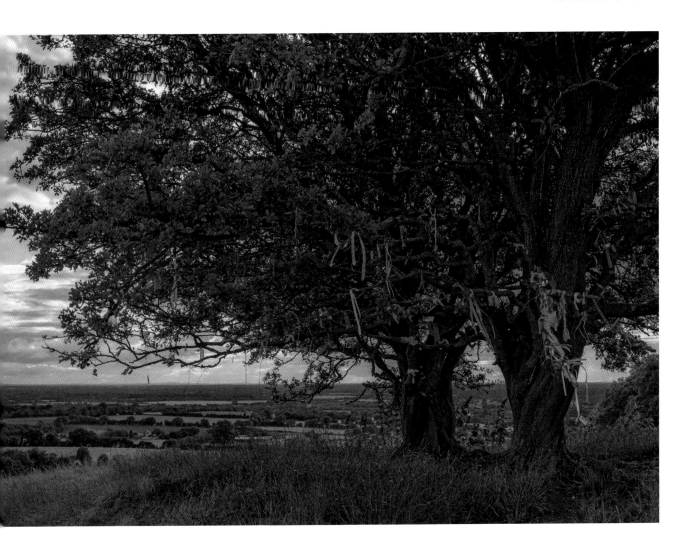

Right beside the King's Seat lies another mound which is known as Cormac's House; Cormac reigned as king from 220 AD to 260 AD and hovers between legend and history; his name is credited with composing the ancient Brehon Laws of Ireland and his time of reign coincides with the legend of the great Fionn Mac Cumhaill and the Fianna.

Surrounding the Mound of Hostages, the King's Seat and Cormac's House is an enclosure known as the Rath of Kings (*Rath na Ríogh*). The Rath of Kings dates from before the time of Christ and is thought to have been a spiritual monument rather than a defensive structure.

Outside the Rath of Kings lies the Rath of Synods (despite being named after early Christian church assemblies, this is also pre Christian); Gráinne's Fort, named after the daughter of Cormac, the Sloping Trenches (which look like two forts sliding down the hill) and the Banqueting Hall (which was probably, in fact, an entranceway).

The legends also note that the five great roads of Ireland had their junction here at Tara: The Asail Way to the north west; The Great Way to the west that divided Ireland into two; The Dhala Way to the south west; The Cualann Way to the south by Dublin and Wicklow Mountains; The Mhidh-luachra Way to the north and Ulster all fanned out from here at Tara.

The actual Banqueting Hall that hosted the guests of the Great Gathering or Féis that happened every three years at Tara is now thought to have been located somewhere else on the hill. During the Féis, laws were made, athletic contests took place and of course there was much storytelling, music and feasting.

In the *Book of Leinster* the Banqueting Hall was described as being three hundred feet in length and that it had 150 sections with fifty guests in each. The book further describes that 'thrice fifty steaming cooks' were needed to prepare the food and three hundred men were needed to serve it. It must have been quite a party!

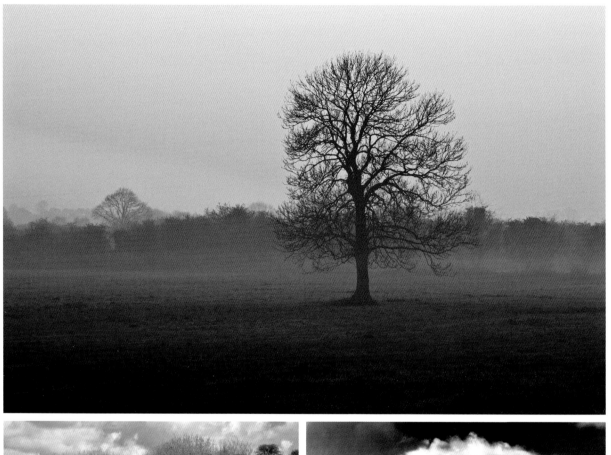

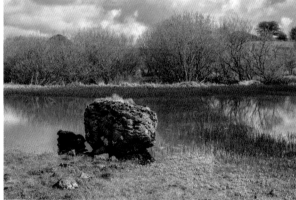

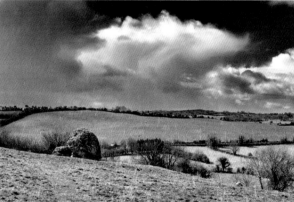

Left page top: Winter Dawn, Co. Westmeath
Left page bottom left: Lough Lugh, Hill of Uisneach, Co. Westmeath
Left page bottom right: Catstone, Hill of Uisneach, Co. Westmeath
Right page: Fairy Tree, Hawthorn, Hill of Uisneach, Co. Westmeath

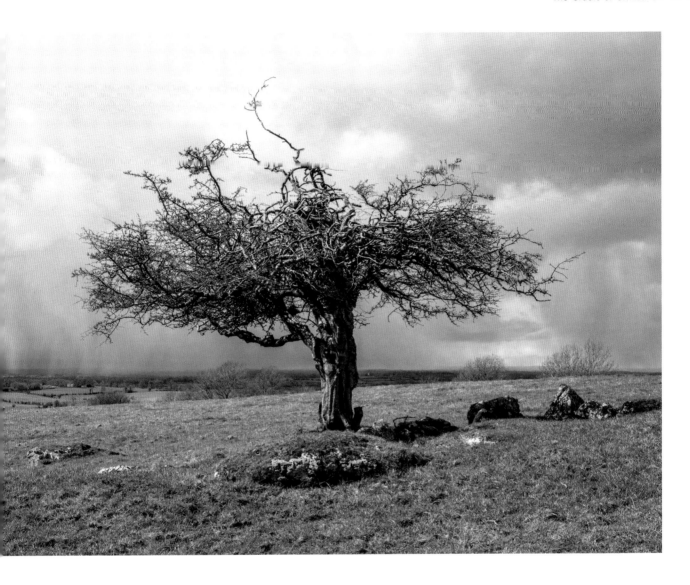

The Hill of Uisneach stands more or less in the exact centre of Ireland and rises some 180 metres above the surrounding countryside. Uisneach intricately interweaves mythology and history, legend and actual events are impossible to tell apart.

The oldest signs of human activity date back to Neolithic times, but it is very likely that Uisneach was a sacred place even before that time period. In the times of the Celts Uisneach was believed to be the gateway to a mythical fifth province, *Mide*, the magical Otherworld, which holds together the four provinces of the real world, Munster, Connaught, Ulster and Leinster. *Mide* however also represents a real place: County Meath, at the time one of the main kingdoms of Ireland.

The mythical fifth province was accessed through the Stone of Divisions *Aill na Mireann* a massive glacial erratic made of fissured and fragmented limestone. This thirty tonne boulder was also known as *Umbilicus Hiberniae* and *Axis Mundi*, the Navel of Ireland, and is today widely known as the Catstone. The historic status of the Catstone made it an assembly point

even in recent history: Daniel O'Connell, Eamon De Valera and Pádraig Pearse all choose this site to address their followers during political rallies.

Uisneach was believed to be the home of the Earth goddess, Eriu, after whom Ireland ('Land of Eriu') was named and who according to legend rests under the Catstone. The sun god and warrior Lugh, after whom the harvest festival, Lughnasa, was named, also has connections to Uisneach: it is said that he met his end in the lake that carries his name and that he is buried nearby.

Megalithic Tombs, including *St Patrick's Bed* at the very top of the hill and the resting place of Lugh *Lugh's Tumulus*; holy wells and a number of ancient enclosures and ringforts lie in close proximity to each other on the hill. The most impressive of the latter is known as *The Royal Palace* which was likely the seat of a king or chieftain, possibly even the High King of Ireland before the rise of Tara. It consists of an outer wall and the foundations of a number of houses. An ancient roadway that linked Uisneach with Tara leads to the entrance of the Royal Palace.

Left page: Cooley Mountains, Co. Louth
Right page: Countryside near Tallanstown, Co. Louth

The Cooley Peninsula occupies the north eastern corner of County Louth, Ireland's smallest county, also known as 'The Wee County'. The area formed the backdrop for one of the greatest stories in Irish mythology: 'Táin Bó Cúailnge: The Cattle Raid of Cooley'.

The story starts with a heated argument between Maeve, queen of Connaught, and her husband, Ailill, about which of them has more wealth. To settle the argument it was decided to bring together all their possessions in one room and compare. As it turned out they were almost equal. The only item Ailill possessed that Maeve did not was Finnbeannach: a magnificent looking, white-horned bull.

Maeve raged with anger and started to look for a way to get even. The only animal that would match Finnbeannach at the time belonged to Daire Mac Fiachna from Ulster. Maeve sent out messengers with the plea to borrow Daire's Brown Bull of Cooley for a year. After some negotiations Daire finally agreed, but changed his mind at the last minute after hearing rumours that Maeve would have taken the bull by force if necessary.

What followed was one of the greatest mythological battles ever fought in Ireland. The battle was also the grand entrance of Ireland's mightiest hero: Cú Chulainn. He was the one who single-handedly held Maeve's forces at bay, slaughtering thousands of her warriors, as it was promised by the fortune-teller Fedelm:

I see him moving to the fray:
Take warning, watch him well,
Cú Chulainn, Sualdam's son!
Now I see him in pursuit.

Whole hosts he will destroy,
making dense massacre.
In thousands you will yield your heads.
I am Fedelm. I hide nothing.

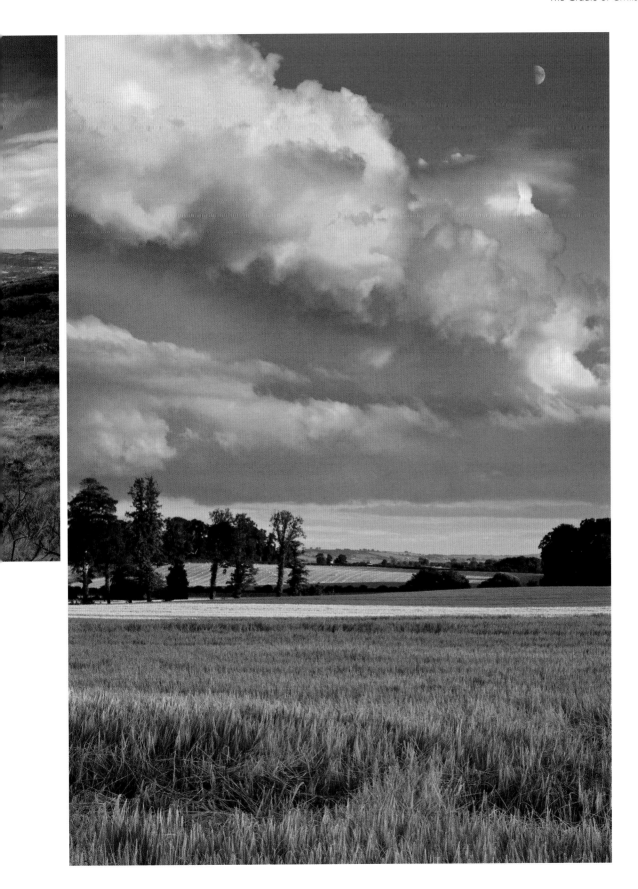

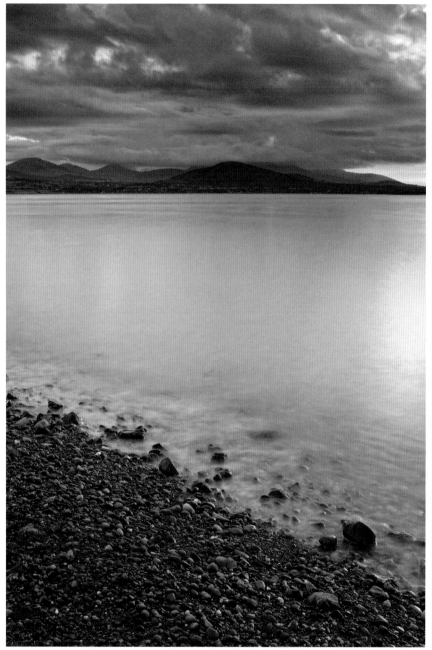
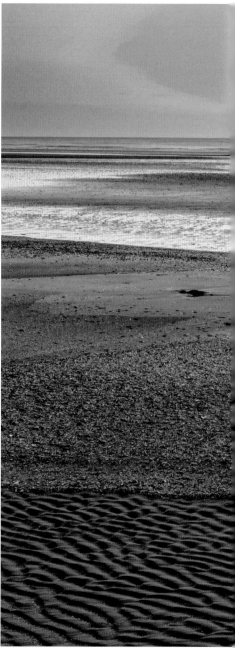

Left page: Carlingford Lough and Mourne Mountains, Co. Louth
Right page: Port Strand Sunrise, Co. Louth

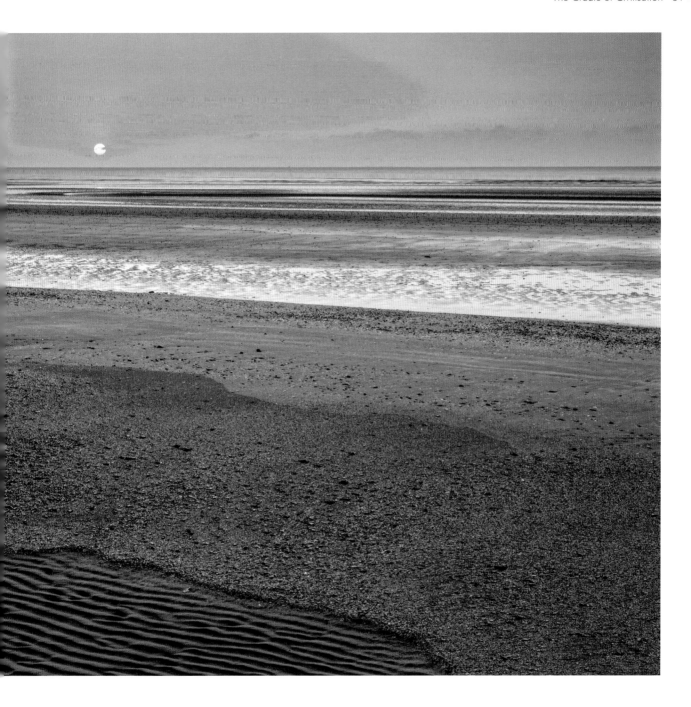

The final engagement was between Cú Chulainn and his foster brother, Ferdia, who fought on Maeve's side. It is said the battle raged for five days with the opponents being equally matched as well as reluctant to hurt each other. On the fifth day Ferdia managed to pierce Cú Chulainn's chest with his sword and Cú Chulainn retaliated with his *Gae Bolga*, a magical spear that could penetrate any armour; Ferdia died instantly.

In the meantime Maeve had managed to grab the bull and was holding the animal in her camp, but she was still trapped in Ulster. A final battle broke out and although Maeve had to retreat she managed to bring the bull with her.

Back in her own kingdom it was decided the two bulls should fight each other. The brutal battle lasted all day and night and when the second day dawned the Brown Bull of Cooley was seen walking towards his own lands with the bloody remains of Finnbeannach hanging from his horns.

Maeve and Ailill made peace with each other and peace with Ulster and so the story ends.

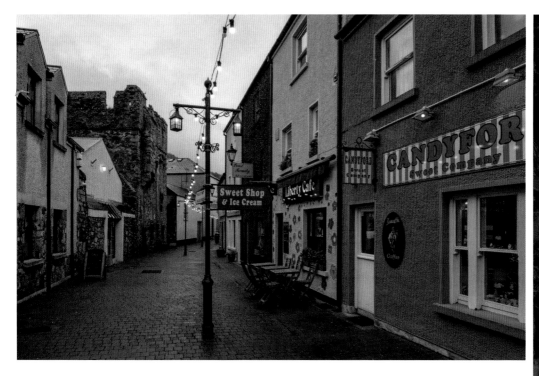
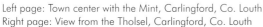

Left page: Town center with the Mint, Carlingford, Co. Louth
Right page: View from the Tholsel, Carlingford, Co. Louth

CASTLES AND CONQUESTS

Carlingford lies on the northern shores of the Cooley Peninsula overlooking Carlingford Lough and the Mourne Mountains across the water. It is one of the best-preserved medieval towns in Ireland and walking the streets is a bit like entering a time machine.

King John's Castle is the most prominent building in the town. It was finished around 1261 in a strategic position on the edge of Carlingford Lough and was the first line of defence against invaders for some four hundred years. Before the Normans settled at Carlingford Lough however it is thought that the area served as a temporary base for Viking raiders. Carlingford derives from the Scandinavian 'Fjord of Carlinn' and although no factual evidence for Viking presence has been recovered so far it is taken as a given that the Vikings lived at the lough before the Normans arrived in 1184. The town that grew in the shadow of the King John's

Castle flourished during the fourteenth, fifteenth and early sixteenth centuries and, at the time, was one of the most important trading posts of the wider area.

Many of the typical features of a medieval trading town are still present. Parts of the original town wall are still standing as is the Tholsel, a tollgate where taxes were levied on all kinds of goods entering the town. The Mint is a fifteenth-century fortified tower house that was built by one of Carlingford's wealthy merchants. The nearby Taaffe's Castle, a tower house with an annex for more comfortable living quarters, was built in the 16th century by the Earl of Carlingford, Nicholas Taaffe who fell at the Battle of the Boyne in 1690.

Nicholas's death marked the end of one of the most tragic Irish love stories. Nicholas fell in love with a servant girl named Eimear. It was

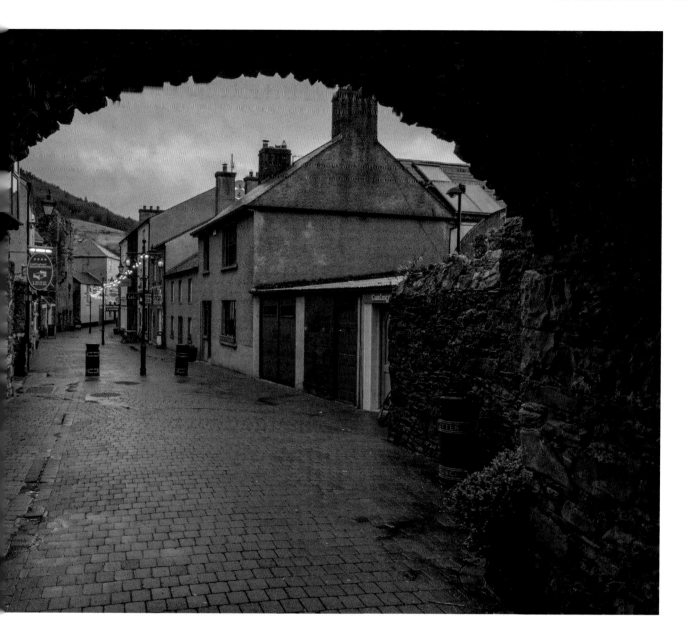

love at first sight on both sides despite their different social standings. Nicholas asked Eimear for her hand in marriage and a date was set for 14 July 1690. Only a few days after the proposal Nicholas was called to arms. Eimear's last words to Nicholas were 'I will never forsake you, I will forever wait for your return.'

On 12 July 1690 Nicholas was killed, pierced through the heart and beheaded. The last words he spoke were to cry out her name.

When the news reached Carlingford Eimear, who had been alone in her room for days, was found dead on the floor, showing the same injuries as Nicholas: she was bleeding from her heart, her head was severed from her body. The horrified staff sealed the room with Eimear inside. She was never buried and until this day she haunts Taaffe's Castle waiting for Nicholas to return.

Another medieval building is the Dominican Friary, first established in 1305 under the patronage of Richard de Burgo, Earl of Ulster. It was dissolved in 1540 by Henry VIII of England. In 1670 the Dominicans, as well us the Franciscans wanted to return to the friary. The resuling dispute was eventually settled in favour of the Dominicans who stayed there until the eighteenth century.

Carlingford's decline began in the seventeenth century when political unrest and war arrived in Ireland in the shape of Oliver Cromwell. In addition, the major source of income, the herring shoals that were plenty in the lough, had disappeared. In 1744 the town has been described as being in ruins.

This fast decline and lack of any post medieval development resulted in the town retaining much of its medieval structure. At the beginning of the 20th century Reverend Laurence Murray wrote of Carlingford that the town was 'a gold mine to the antiquarian … it is narrow, hilly, angular and gloomy – there is a medieval suggestiveness about it which carries one back many centuries and fills the mind with vague dreamings'.

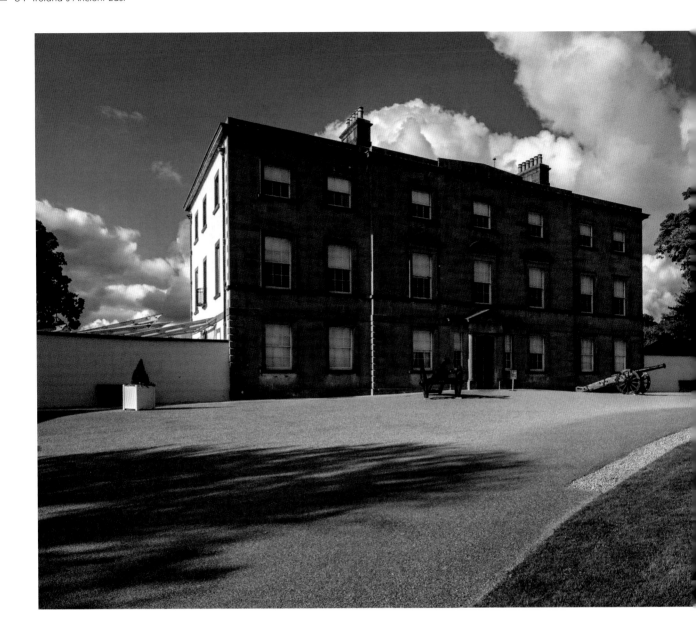

The Battle of the Boyne was one of the greatest military encounters that ever took place on Irish soil. At stake was the English throne and the religious freedom in Ireland.

The Catholic James II had lost throne and power in 1688 to the Protestant William III of England better known as William of Orange who, on a side note, was married to James's daughter Mary II. What followed was a military conflict that lasted for three years and became known as the Williamite-Jacobite War or *Cogadh an Dá Rí*, the War of the Two Kings.

The Battle of the Boyne took place in July of 1690 at the River Boyne near the town of Drogheda. William brought 36,000 men while James had 25,000, mainly Irish Catholics and some French reinforcements.

James II soon ordered the retreat despite some reports that claim that he had the chance to beat William's army. This hasty retreat gave him the nickname '*Séamus a' chaca*', 'James the shit' among the Irish.

The war would then move to the west of Ireland and continue until 1691 when the followers of James II would accept defeat under the Treaty of Limerick and leave Ireland.

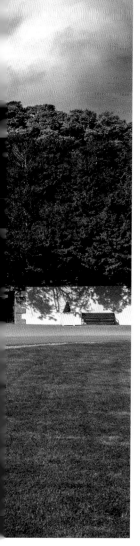

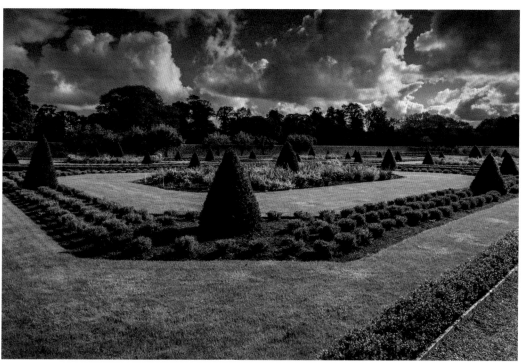

Left page: Oldbridge House, Battle of the Boyne Site, Co. Meath
Right page: Oldbridge House Gardens, Battle of the Boyne Site, Co. Meath

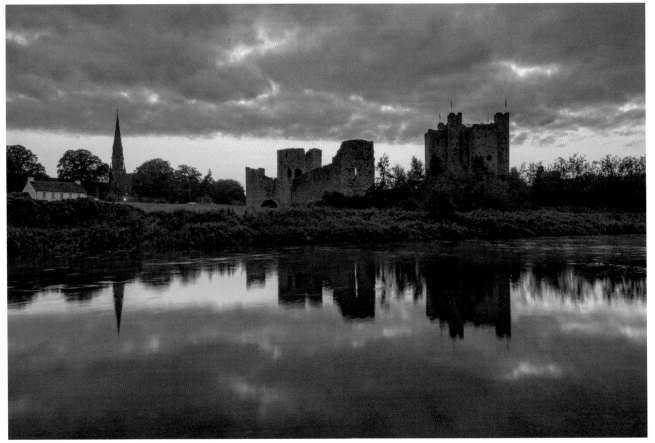

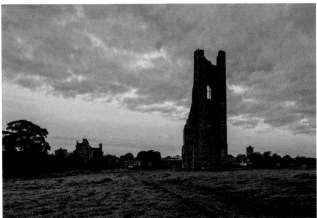

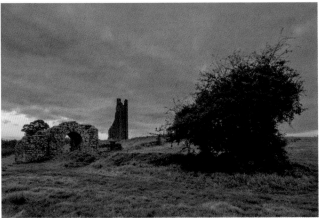

Trim, the 'town at the ford of the elder trees', is said to have been founded either by St Loman who sailed up the Boyne in 433AD and built a church there, or by St Patrick himself who then handed the settlement over to St Loman to move on to other tasks. In any case a bustling town soon grew around the church.

In the late twelfth century, soon after the Norman invasion of Ireland, the lordship of Meath was granted to Baron Hugh De Lacy. De Lacy immediately built a fortification in Trim, at the southern bank of the Boyne. This first castle at Trim was probably built of wood and soon fell victim to the invading forces of Rory O'Connor, King of Connacht. Hugh De Lacy, however, wasn't

that easily overthrown and soon a stronger castle was built, which grew eventually into the Trim Castle of today, the largest and most impressive Anglo-Norman fortification in Ireland. Hugh also took Rose, the daughter of Rory O'Connor, as his second wife. It is however very unlikely this was a marriage of love.

Over the centuries the ownership of the castle changed several times and by the sixteenth century Trim Castle was mainly abandoned, was only used occasionally as a military base and fell into disrepair. Today the castle is partly restored and featured as a 'Scottish' castle in the 1995 movie *Braveheart*.

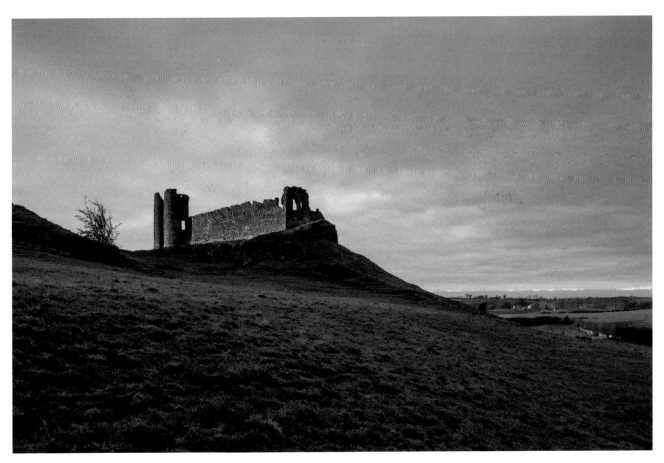

Left page top: River Boyne and Trim Castle, Co. Meath
Left page bottom left: The Yellow Steeple, Trim, Co. Meath
Left page bottom right: Sheep's Gate, Trim, Co. Meath
Right page: Castle Roche, Co. Louth

While the southern banks of the Boyne are still dominated by Trim Castle, the northern banks have their own specila features, like Yellow Steeple, the ruined bell tower of St Mary's Abbey, Talbot's Castle, which was formerly part of the abbey, but was converted into a fourteenth century manor house, and the Sheep's Gate, the only remaining gate of once five that led into the walled town of Trim.

Castle Roche, located east of the Cooley Peninsula, is very similar to its sister castle at Carlingford, but unfortunately much of its history has been lost. What is known is that it was built by Rohesia de Verdon in 1236. Rohesia, after having lost her first husband Theobald le Botiller in France, decided to settle on her lands in Ireland and offered her hand in marriage to anyone who could built a castle to her liking. It is said that the unfortunate soul who succeeded died at the wedding night, pushed out a window by Rohesia herself. His ghost still haunts the ruin and he makes regular appearances in what is now known as the 'Murder Window'.

Left page: Church and Graveyard, Hill of Slane, Co. Meath
Right page top: The Unfinished Cross and Round Tower, Kells, Co. Meath
Right page bottom: The West Cross / The Broken Cross, Kells, Co. Meath

SACRED IRELAND

The Hill of Slane just north of the village of the same name rises 158 metres above the plains of County Meath and plays an important part in Christian history. According to Muirchu Moccu Mactheni's *Life of Patrick*, written in the 7th century, the Hill of Slane was where Patrick lit his first Paschal fire to defy the pagan kings of Ireland. This happened in 433 AD during the pagan festival of Bealtaine, which was celebrated at the nearby Hill of Tara. The king at the time who was being described as 'fierce and pagan' had strictly forbidden any fires within the view of Tara during the festival, but he was so impressed by Patrick's devotion and his courage to defy him that he allowed Patrick to continue his mission.

Today the Hill of Slane features the ruins of a friary dating from 1512, a gothic tower and a college. The latter has been established by St Erc who was the first bishop of Slane and directly appointed by St Patrick.

Kells is one of the oldest towns in Ireland. The site at the River Blackwater is thought to have been a royal settlement with connections to the Hill of Tara since prehistoric times. In 804AD a group of Columban monks arrived after they had left their monastery on the Scottish island of Iona to escape frequent and violent Viking attacks. Soon a town grew around the flourishing monastery. Like many others the monastery at Kells lost importance and disappeared under English rule in the sixteenth century, but the town remained.

What remains of the monastery today is a number of high crosses, a round tower in which, according to legend, Murchadh, King of Tara, was murdered in 1077, and St Colmcille's (also known as Columcille's or Columba's) House, a two-storey oratory from the eleventh century.

Some believe it was in this very oratory that the Book of Kells was finished. The Book of Kells or 'The Great Gospel of Colmcille' is one of the most beautiful and intricate artworks of the early Christian era consisting

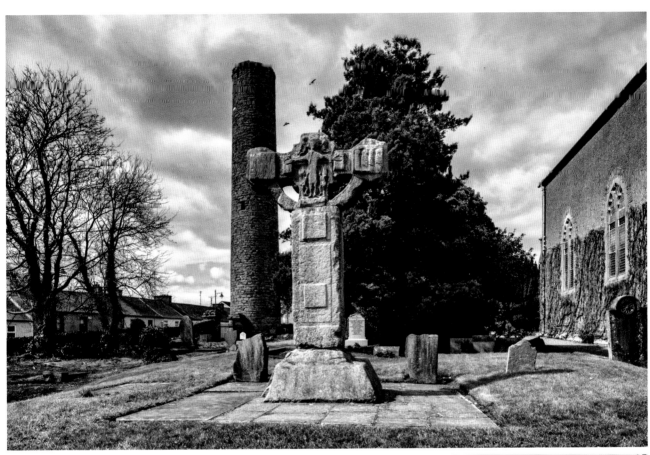

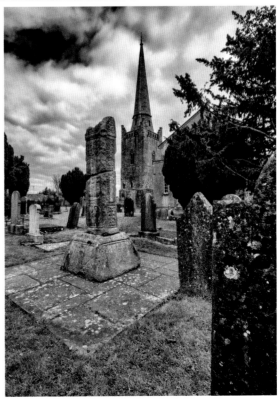

of 680 pages, 340 vellum leaves written and lavishly decorated on both sides. The debate on whether The Book of Kells was made on Iona or Kells, or both is still ongoing. The sources for the rich colours that were used to create the drawings are also a bit of a mystery. Certain local plants and roots have been the base for some colours, others however were based on minerals that could only be sourced in what is today Afghanistan.

What is certain is that a number of monks workedon the manuscript. So far at least three individual styles have been identified and the individuals responsible are known as 'The Goldsmith', 'The Illustrator' and 'The Portrait Painter'. Some of the scribes have also left personal notes like this: 'My only friend is god, I have no drinking cup or goblet but my shoe.'

In 1649 Oliver Cromwell arrived from England for his controversial military campaign and in its wake Bishop Henry Jones of Meath removed the valuable manuscript from Kells, fearing for its safety, and handed it over to Trinity College Dublin where it remains today.

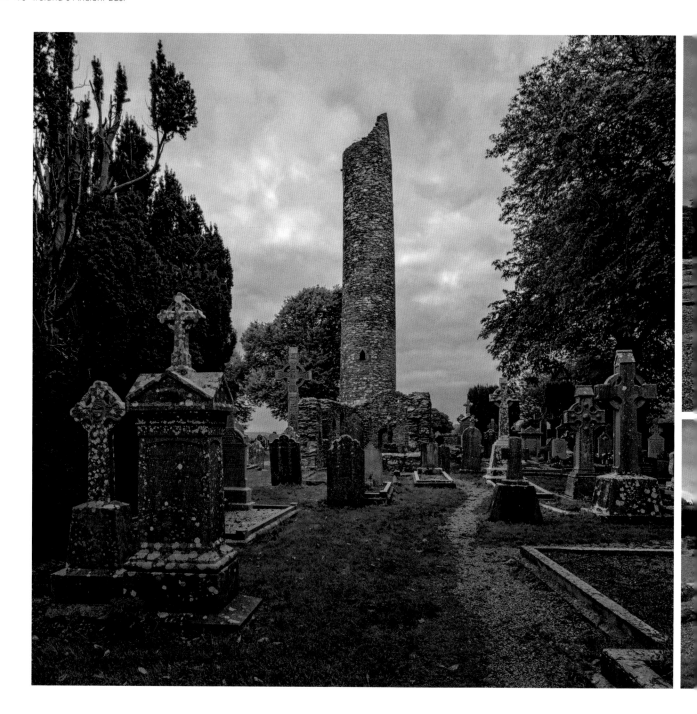

Monasterboice was founded in the fifth century by St Buithe, who gave his name to the River Boyne and, after his death in 520AD, ascended directly into heaven via a ladder lowered from above. Monasterboice was the main centre for spirituality and scholarship until the Cistercians arrived in 1142 to found the nearby Mellifont Abbey. Today, Monasterboice is best known for its High Crosses: The massive Muirdach's Cross, named after the abbot whose name is mentioned in the inscription on the base of the cross, is 5.5 metres tall. The West Cross is more elegant than Muirdach's Cross and, at almost 7 metres, the tallest High Cross in Ireland.

Mellifont Abbey (*An Mhainistir Mhór* – The Big Abbey) was founded in 1142, the first Cistercian Abbey in Ireland. By 1170 Mellifont was home to one hundred monks and three hundred lay brothers. Today little remains of the original buildings, but the Cistercian Order returned in 1938 and founded a New Mellifont at Oriel Temple, Collon close to the original site.

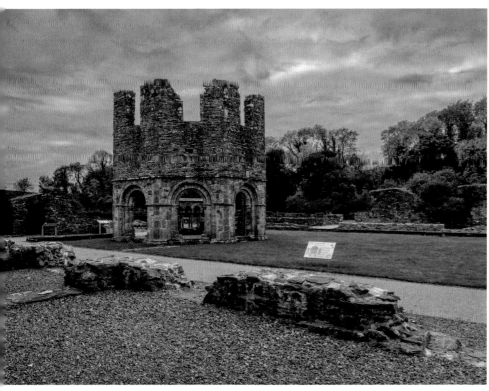

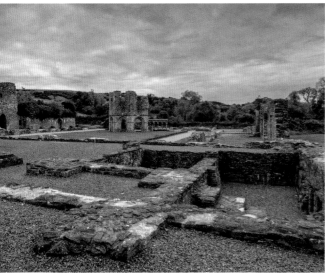

Left page: Monasterboice, Co. Louth
Right page top: The Lavabo (Communal Washing Place), Old Mellifont Abbey, Co. Louth
Right page bottom: Old Mellifont Abbey, Co. Louth

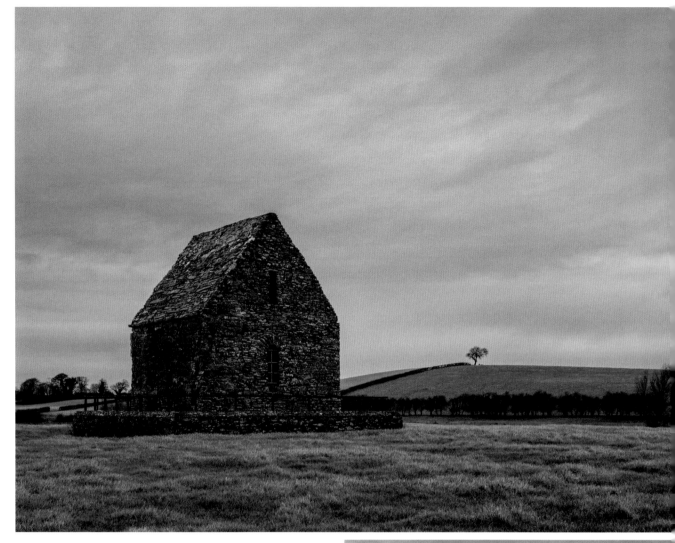

Left page top: St Mochta's House, Louth Village, Co. Louth
Left page bottom: Dromiskin Roundtower and Church, Co. Louth
Right page: Bishop's Bedell's Sycamore, Kilmore, Co. Cavan

It is said that this Sycamore Tree (right) was planted by Bishop Bedell of Kilmore and Ardagh. Bedell was born in England in 1571 and appointed Provost of Trinity College, Dublin in 1627 and took on his post as bishop in 1629. Unusually for an English cleric he treated Protestants and Catholics alike and supported the use of the Irish language. Together with the Rector of nearby Templeport parish, Muircheartach Ó Cionga, he translated the Old Testament into Irish.

During the Irish rebellion of 1641 he provided shelter to both Protestant and Catholic refugees, which made him eventually a target for the rebel forces. When he refused to hand over refugees the rebels stormed Bedell's house and seized him and a number of others.

Bedell was kept prisoner and tortured for a number of weeks. When the rebellion started to subside he was released but died from his wounds on 7 February 1642. The words spoken at the funeral by the Catholic priest Father Farrelly sum up Bedell's status in the community: *May my soul be with Bedell's*

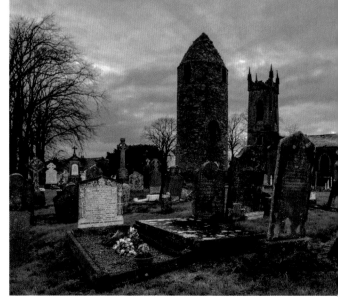

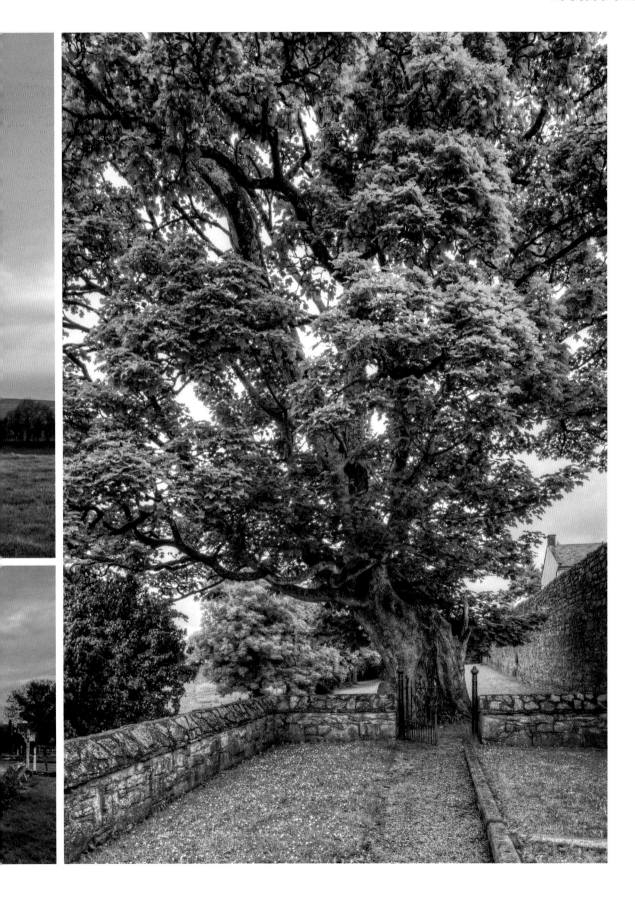

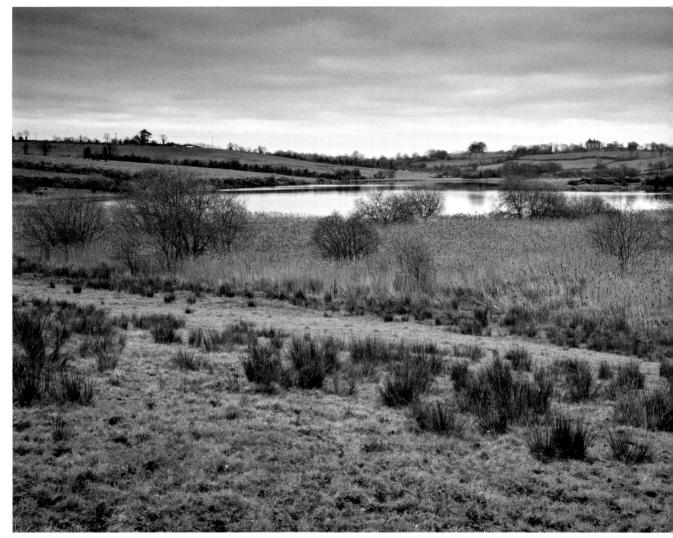

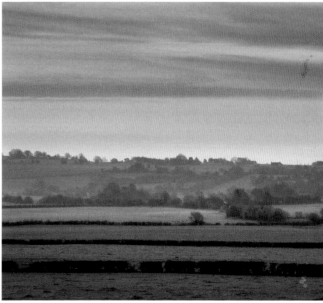

Left page top: Annaghmakerrig Lough, Co. Cavan
Left page bottom: Fields and Hedgerows, Co. Westmeath
Right page: Abbeylara Monastery, Co. Westmeath

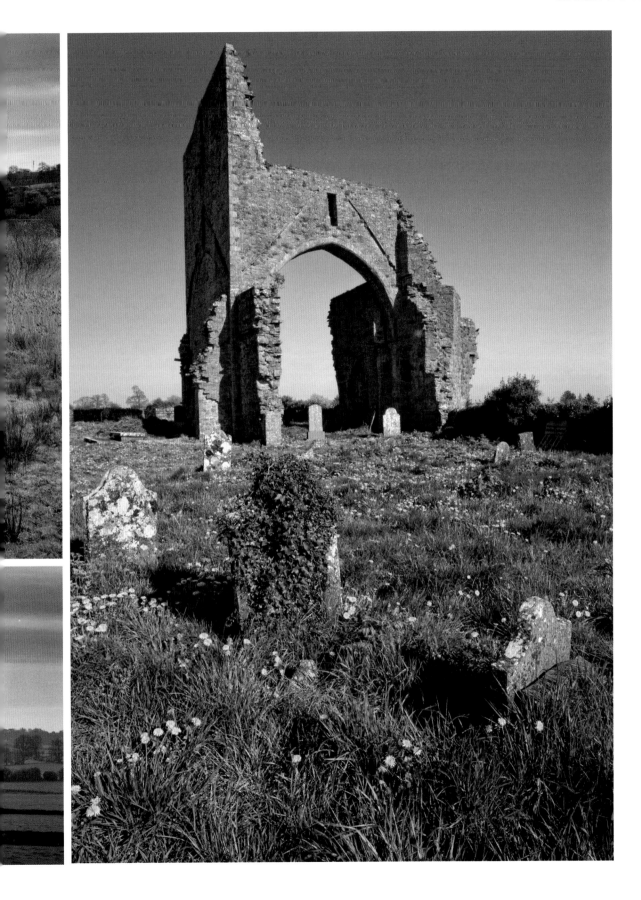

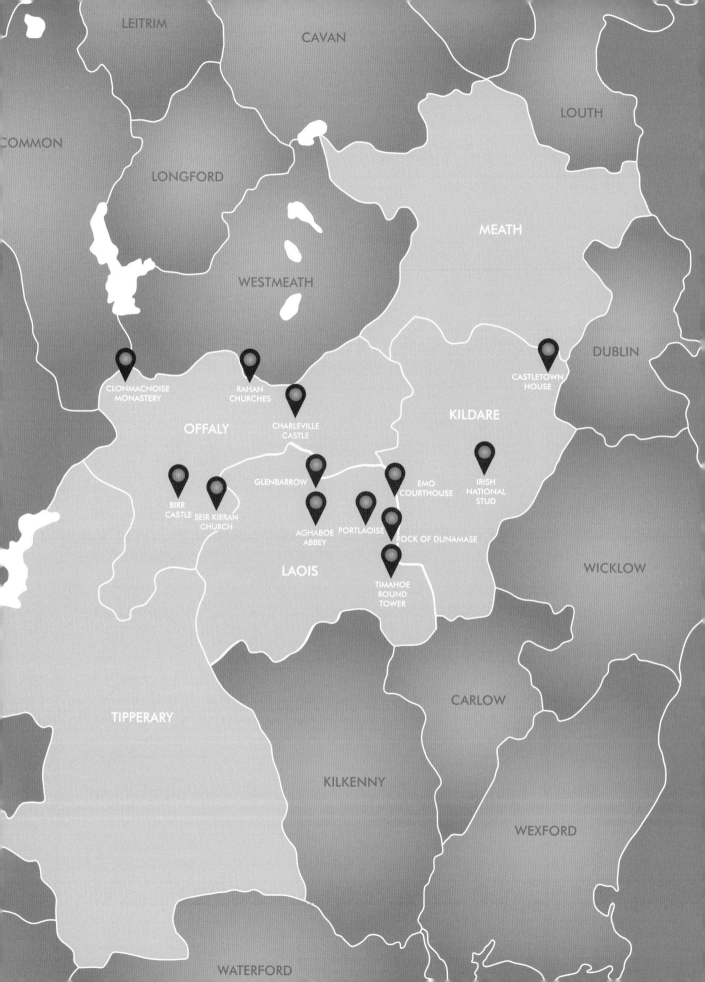

LAND OF THE MONASTERIES

The first missionaries to Ireland most likely came from Gaul (present-day France) in the 4th century, but their work was confined to the south and east of Ireland and left only a small impact. By the 5th century the Irish were not only trading with, but also raiding, parts of Britain and establishing colonies in Scotland and Wales and it was then that Christianity found its way to Ireland.

One name, of course, is synonymous with bringing the Christian faith to Ireland: St Patrick. Patrick was born as 'Patricius' in north western Britain and at the age of sixteen was seized by Irish pirates and sold into slavery. For six years he was forced to herd sheep and cattle in the loneliness of County Mayo and during these dark times in his life he turned to God. One night God spoke to him, ordering him to return to his homeland across the Irish Sea. Patrick made the arduous journey, was welcomed home by his parents and settled into a new life of worship and study. But he couldn't forget the time he had spent in Ireland and one night he dreamed of a man coming to him with many letters. The man handed one of those letters to Patrick. The words in the letter turned into the voices of the people he had known in Ireland, calling him to come back. The letter is known as *Vox Hiberniae*, 'The Voice of the Irish'. Patrick saw this as his calling to travel back to Ireland and spread the word of God. The rest is, as the saying goes, history. Patrick returned to Ireland, banished the metaphorical snakes and became the country's patron saint.

Other missionaries were active in Ireland at the same time as Patrick; while Patrick concentrated his activities on the northern parts of the country the southern half was left to others: St Secundius, St Auxilius, and St Isernius among.

Within two centuries of the arrival of the first missionaries, the Christian faith had replaced the pagan belief system and a major change was on the way. By the early 6th century the first monasteries had been established and many more would follow. A cluster of these monasteries came into being in the heart of Ireland, between the river Shannon in the west and the Slieve Bloom Mountains in the east. At that time the area was covered in uncultivated bog, lakes and ponds, crossed by a few rivers. The only means to travel across this landscape were wooden roads ('toghers') or to follow glacial ridges, known as 'eskers'. These eskers became the main roads across the country from east to west and the first monasteries were established along these important routes. St Columba founded Durrow at Slighe More ('Great Road') and St. Cieran settled at the Eska Riada ('Dividing Road').

These monasteries were the foundation of the Golden Age in Ireland. They grew into centres for learning, art and trade and some became so famous they attracted scholars and students from all across Europe. While the continent descended into the dark ages after the demise of the Roman Empire, Ireland became a shining beacon of scholarship and art. During this time the famous high crosses, like the ones at Monasterboice, were carved and manuscripts like the Book of Kells were written.

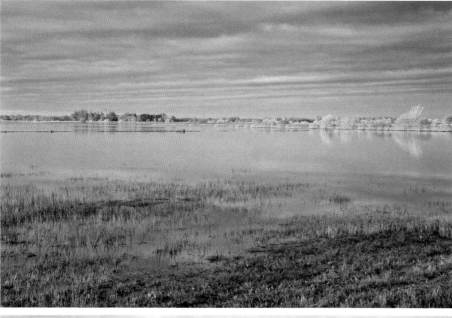

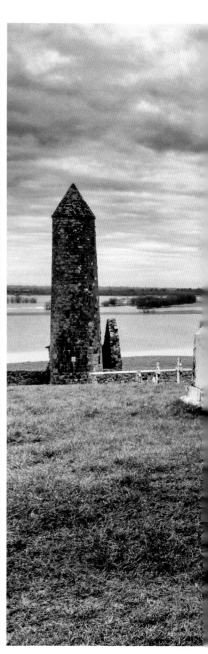

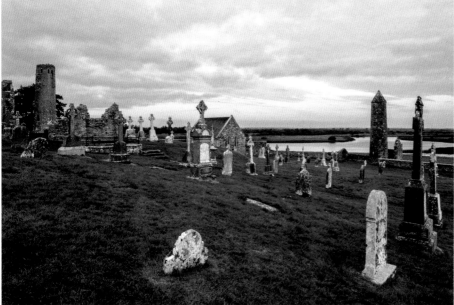

IRELAND'S MYSTICAL WATERWAY

Clonmacnoise occupies one of the most scenic locations in Ireland where the river Shannon winds its way through a gentle landscape of meadows and hedgerows.

The monastery was founded by St Cieran in 544 AD. Colum Cille, another well-known saint, who attended the famous monastery and school of St Finnian together with Cieran wrote about him:

Noble the youth who goes westward from us.
Cieran, the son of a carpenter;
Without envy, without pride, without contantion,
Without jealousy, without satire.

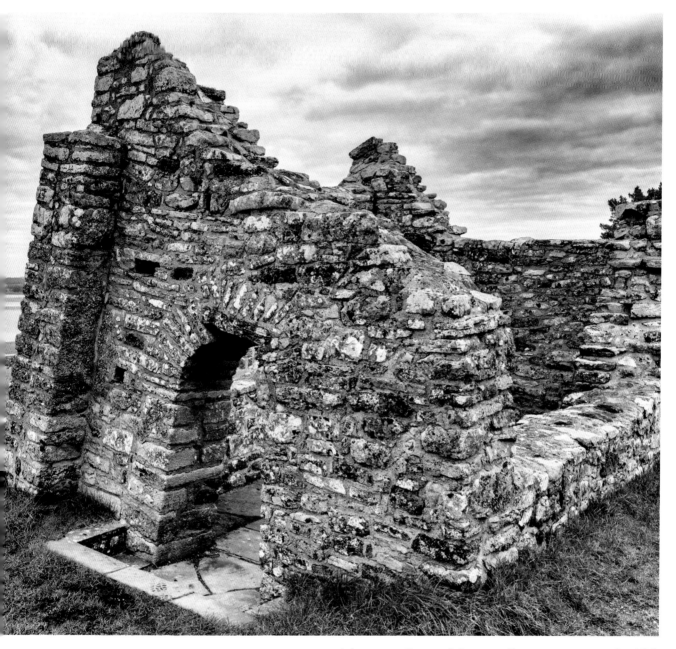

Left page top: Shannon Callows near Clonmacnoise in winter, Co. Offaly
Left page bottom: Clonmacnoise, Co. Offaly
Right page: Temple Cieran, Clonmacnoise, Co. Offaly

The name 'Clonmacnoise' derives either from 'Cluain Maccu Nois' ('Meadow of the sons of Nos') or 'Cluan Mhic Nois' ('Meadow of the pigs of Nos'), which suggests a settlement in the location that predates any Christian activity.

The monastery was founded at the meeting point of two important routes: the river Shannon and the Eska Riada, the main east-west passage and one of the major ancient roads in Ireland. It also lies at the border of three ancient kingdoms, Southern Uí Neill (today's Co. Meath) to the east, Munster to the south and Connaught to the west. This made the monastery an easy target for the neighbouring kingdoms.

Unfortunately Cieran didn't get a chance to see what would become of his humble monastery that only consisted of a few wooden churches at his time. Cieran died of the plague within a year of establishing Clonmacnoise. His early death, however, might have been one of the reasons for the success of his foundation. Almost immediately after his passing a cult began to emerge around him. Tales of his personality and devotion and the fact that both Cieran and Jesus Christ were sons of carpenters and died at the age of thirty-three made Clonmacnoise a special place and attractive to aristocracy and common folk alike.

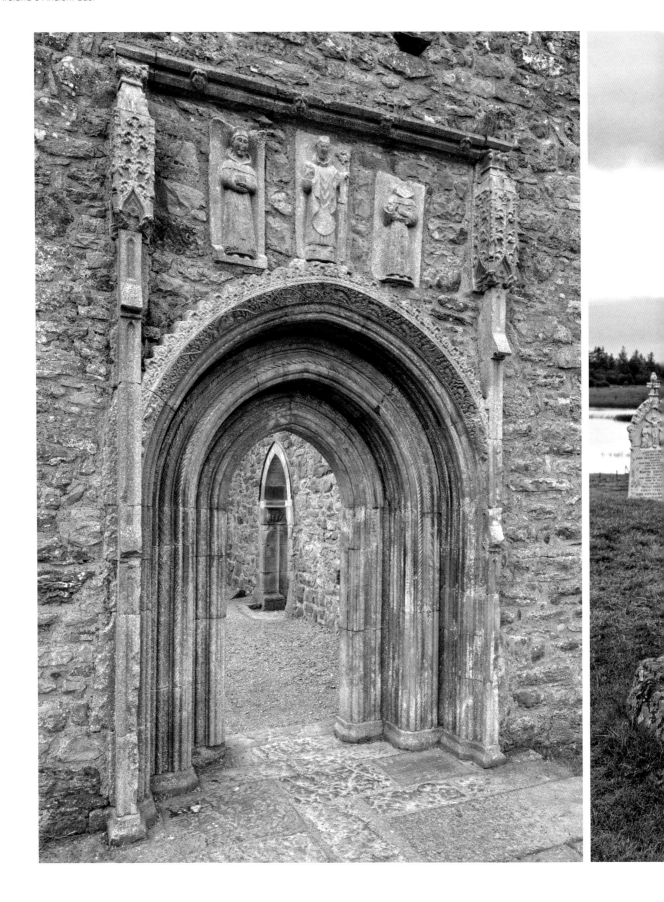

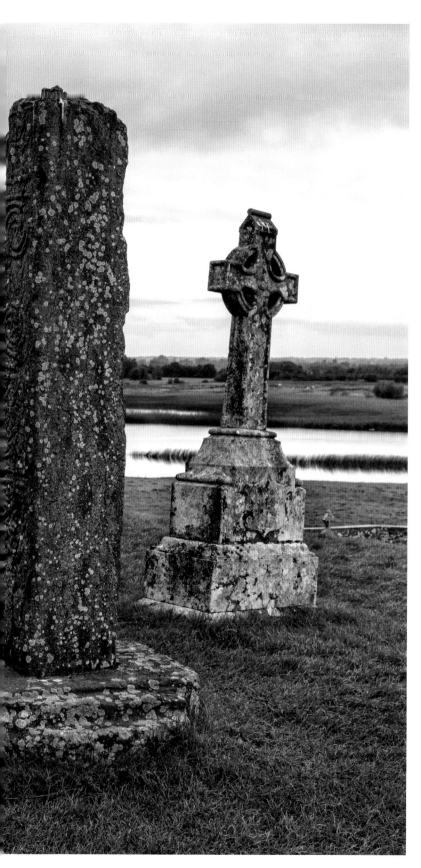

Over the centuries Clonmacnoise became a centre for literature and art; students flocked from all over Europe to study. Hundreds of monks lived and worked at Clonmacnoise producing some of Ireland's most enduring artworks in metal and stone. The wealth that came with this development would drive the economy of the entire region and, at its height around the 8th and 9th century, the monastery would have been surrounded by a large settlement, the ancient city of Clonmacnoise. An archaeological survey discovered the remains of an enormous wooden bridge next to the monastery. This bridge across the Shannon measured 120 metres in length, was 5 metres wide and more than 10 metres high. This bridge not only crossed the Shannon, but also connected the kingdoms of Meath and Connaught, linking the east with the west.

The accumulating material wealth, however, not only threatened to overwhelm the spiritual role of the monastery, it also made Clonmacnoise a target for raids. Over a period of three hundred years Clonmacnoise was raided and burned 35 times by rival Irish kings, the Vikings and later the Anglo-Normans.

From the 12th century onwards the importance of Clonmacnoise began to decline. The repeated raids and a reform of the Church (known as the Gregorian movement) and later the suppression of the Catholic faith by the English crown took its toll. By the late 1600s Clonmacnoise had become a collection of monastic ruins.

After its decline Clonmacnoise became a place of pilgrimage and remained a secret stronghold for the Catholic community especially during the times of the Penal Laws when it was forbidden for Catholics to practise their faith.

The pilgrimage route at Clonmacnoise is known as The Long Station, a walk of penitence and prayer around the buildings of Cieran's shining city and is still practised by many every year on the first Sunday in September.

Left page: Door of the Cathedral,
Clonmacnoise, Co. Offaly
Right page: Standing Stone,
Clonmacnoise, Co. Offaly

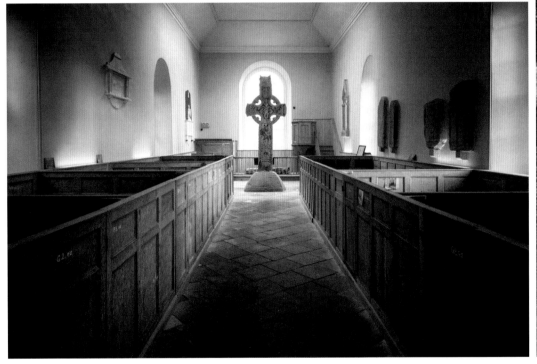

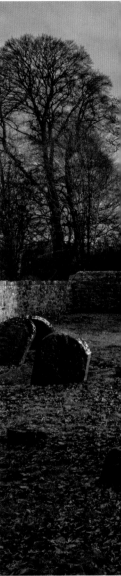

Durrow (The Plain of the Oaks) was founded in 553AD by St. Columba, also known as Colum Cille, and is associated with one of the most famous ancient manuscripts: The Book of Durrow was created sometime between 650 and 700AD. The place of origin has been discussed for decades without consent: Iona, Lindisfarne and Durrow are likely candidates, but the only sure fact is that the manuscript was in Durrow by 916AD.

Columba was born in 521AD in Gartan, County Donegal into a royal family and was himself a successor to the throne. Destiny, however, had other plans. Columba was fostered by a local priest from a very early age and from there he went on to study at various monasteries and eventually surrendered his royal claims and became a monk at Glasnevin. From there, he went out into the world and by the age of 25 he had founded 27 monasteries in Ireland.

Sometime around 560AD Columba's life changed forever. He entered into a quarrel with St Finnian of Movilla Abbey about a copy of a psalter he had copied and intended to keep for himself. In Finnian's opinion the copy belonged to him because he owned the original. It was one of the first copyright disputes in history. After King Diarmuid ruled in favour of Finnian and after another incident where the king, in Columba's opinion, had violated the right of sanctuary, Columba instigated a rebellion against the king, which resulted in the Battle of Cúl

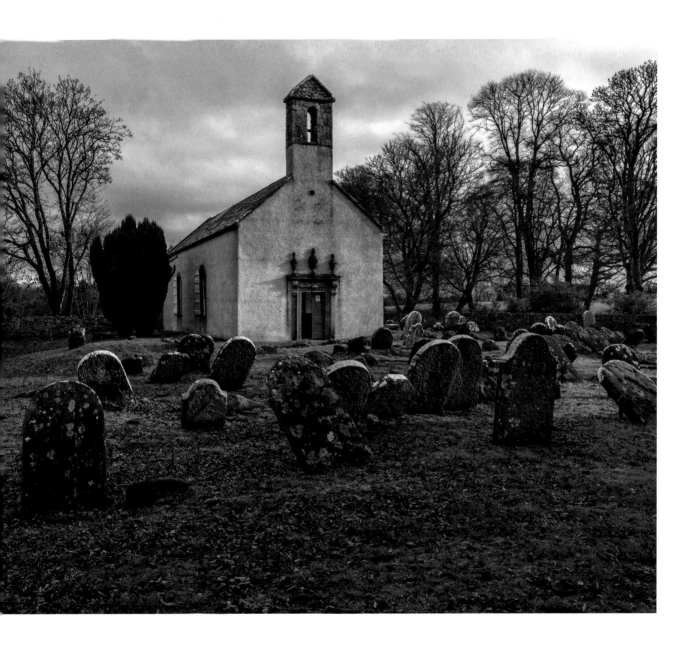

Dreimhne (also known as the battle of the book). The battle was claimed to have caused some three thousand casualties.

To do penance for the deaths he had caused, columba went into exile to scotland with the goal of winning as many souls for christ as had perished in the battle of the book. From his new base on the island of iona he led missions all over scotland and established many more monasteries. It was on Iona that one of the most celebrated ancient manuscripts was started: the Book of Kells. Together with the Book of Durrow, the Book of Kells rests today at the Trinity College, Dublin.

Left page: Durrow Church and High Cross, Co. Offaly
Right page: Durrow Church and graveyard, Co. Offaly

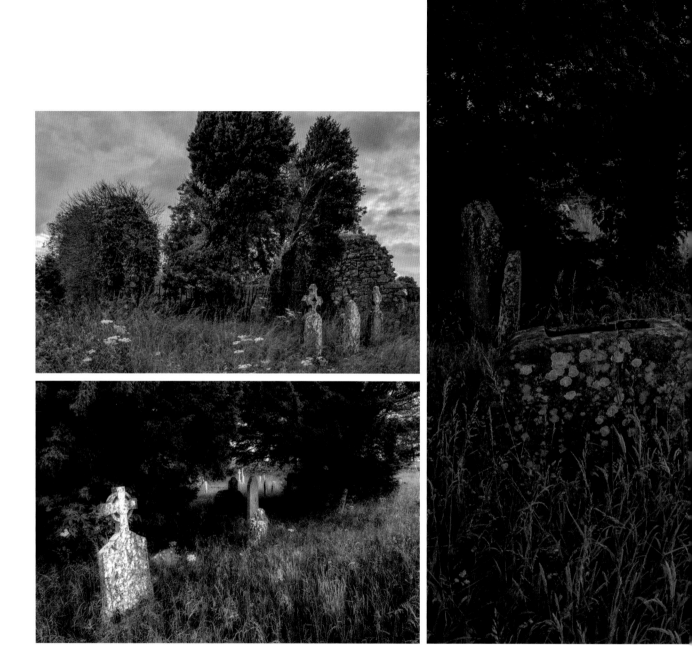

Seirkieran, one of the oldest and most impressive religious communities in Ireland, was founded by no other than St Cieran around or – according to some sources – even before the time of St Patrick.

One of the more popular legends tells us that St Patrick revealed the future site of the monastery to a rather unsure Cieran. Patrick handed a bell to Cieran with the words: 'Thou shalt take my bell, and it will be dumb till it reaches the chosen site, and it will ring when it reaches it.' Patrick went on promising Cieran that 'mighty deeds and miracles will be done by you'.

Seirkieran indeed grew into one of the largest monasteries that ever existed in Ireland and also became the burial place for the kings of Ossory. Remains of the ancient enclosure can still be seen today: a D-shaped earthen bank surrounds some 20 acres.

After St Cieran's death, Seirkieran continued to prosper. Around 1170 the monks adopted the Rule of St Augustine and the walls of the priory built around the same time can still be seen in the graveyard today.

In 1548 the priory was 'burned and destroyed by the English and O'Carroll' (Annals of the Four Masters) and eventually surrendered to the English in 1568.

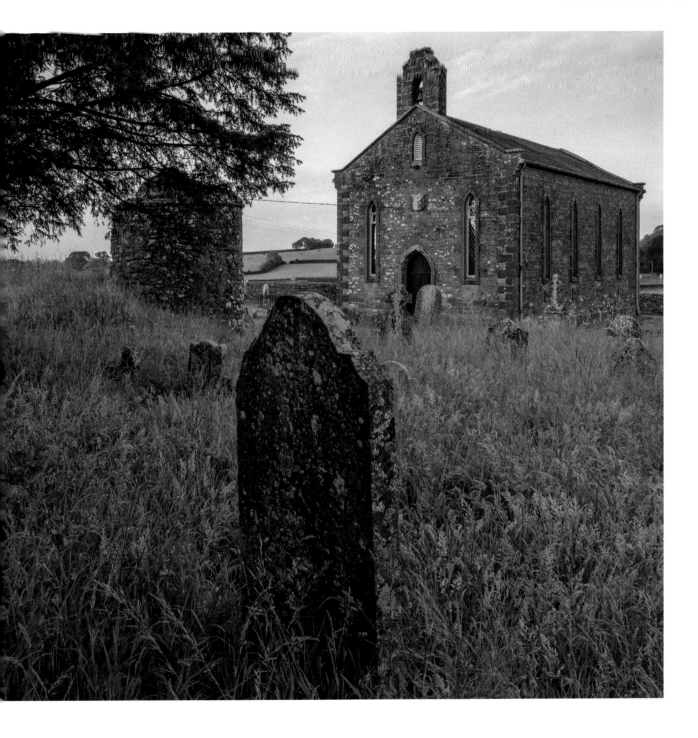

Left page top: Remains of the priory at Seirkieran, Co. Offaly
Left page bottom: Seirkieran Graveyard, Co. Offaly
Right page: Seirkieran, Co. Offaly

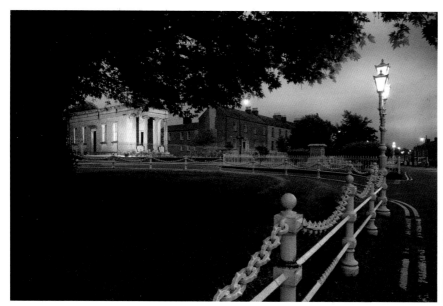

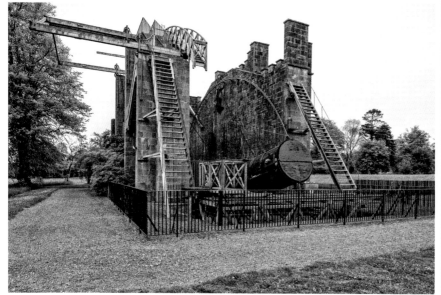

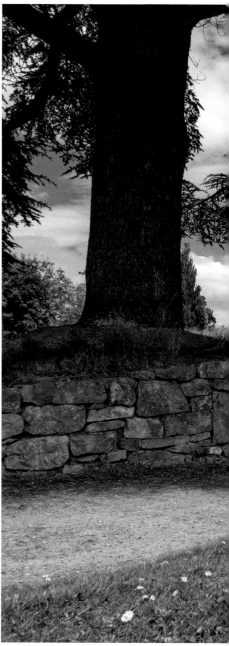

Birr is a market town situated at the meeting of the Camcor and Little Brosna River close to the centre of Ireland. Its origins go back to an early Christian monastery that was founded by St Brendan the Elder in the 6th century. Nothing, however, remains of this monastery and its exact location is unknown.

What is now south Offaly and north Tipperary was once known as 'Ely O'Carroll' or 'Eile Uí Chearbhail' after the O'Carroll clan who ruled the area for generations. The first castle in Birr, most likely a tower-house-style building, is thought to have been built around 1170 and from the 14th to 17th century Birr Castle was one of the O'Carroll's major strongholds. From the late 16th century the clan steadily lost power because of internal feuds and conflicts with neighbouring clans. The tightening grip of the English did the rest and in 1605 the O'Carroll

land was confiscated and given to Jacobean and Cromwellian plantation families.

In 1620 Birr and the land around the town was granted to Sir Laurence Parsons who became the First Earl of Rosse. When he took possession of his new earldom he refused to live in the original O'Carroll tower house and instead moved into the gate house, which was developed into the main residence for his family. The original tower house was destroyed in 1778. The Second Earl of Rosse developed the new castle further and was also very much involved into the planning of the town including the churches and Georgian malls that are still a main feature of Birr today.

William Parsons, the Third Earl of Rosse, a keen astronomer, built what would carry the title of the largest telescope in the world for over 70 years. The 'Great Telescope' was completed in 1845 and with it

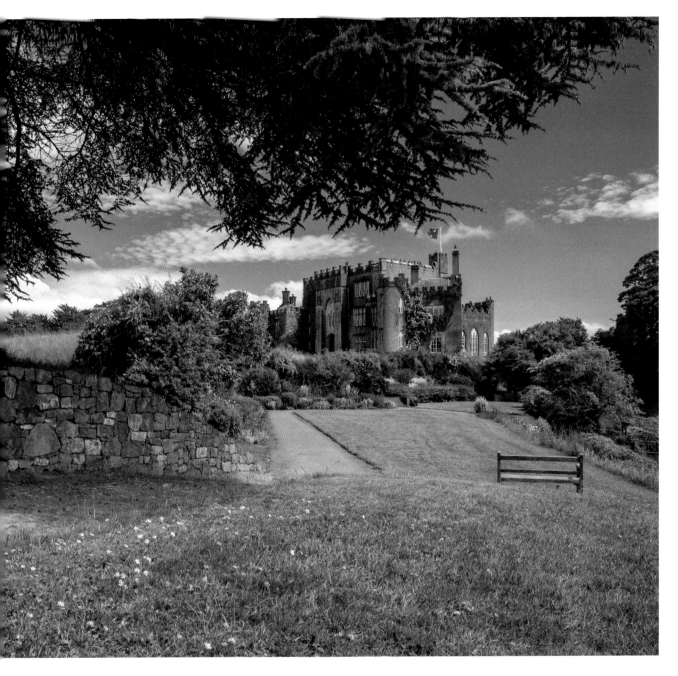

William Parsons discovered the spiral nature of certain nebulae, which led to their identification as galaxies. William's son Laurence, the Fourth Earl of Rosse continued his father's work and even built a second smaller telescope. Laurence and his mother were also eminent photographers and their darkroom, which has been preserved, is thought to be the oldest surviving example in the world. William's youngest son, Charles , made his name as the inventor of the compound steam turbine.

With the Fifth Earl of Rosse interest shifted away from astronomy and science. William Parsons, Fifth Earl of Rosse, introduced plants from all over the world into the garden and in doing this laid the foundation for one of the greatest gardens in Ireland. Among the many exotic and native plants flourishing at Birr Gardens are 300 year old box hedges which are, according to the Guinness Book of Records, the tallest in the world. A grey poplar, some 200 years old and at 42 metres the tallest of its kind in Ireland, fell victim to a storm in 2013. The vast gardens also feature the oldest wrought iron bridge in Ireland dating from 1820.

Brendan, the 7th Earl of Ross, and his wife Allison opened Birr to the public in 2014 and run the estate together with their son Patrick, Lord of Oxmantown, and his family.

Left page top: Birr, Co. Offaly
Left page bottom: The Great Telescope at Birr Castle, Co. Offaly
Right page: Birr Castle, Co. Offaly

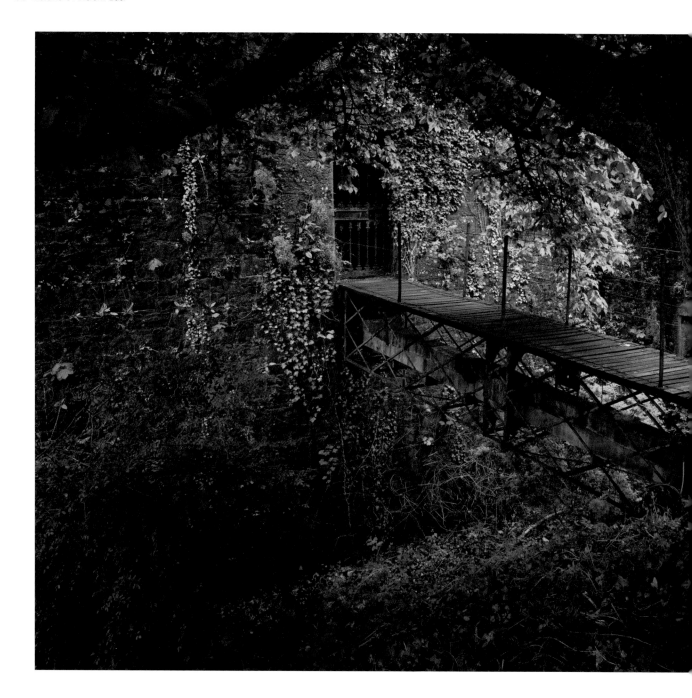

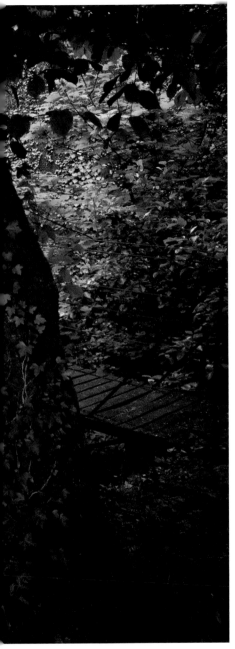

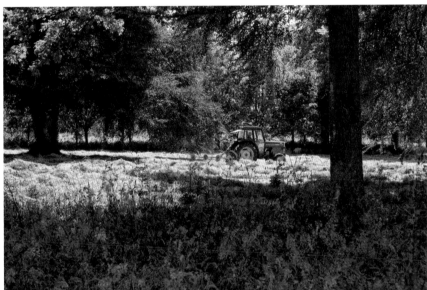

Left page: 'The Back Door', Birr Castle, Co. Offaly
Right page: Making Hay at Birr Castle, Co. Offaly

SACRED IRELAND

Monaincha Abbey has been called 'Tipperary's best kept secret' and it is easy to see why; though it's close to the town of Roscrea and one of Ireland's busiest motorways, it's hidden away behind trees at the end of a small road and stands on a mound in the middle of a field. When the abbey was founded (anywhere between the 6th, 7th or 8th century by either by St Canice of Aghaboe or St Cronan of Roscrea), the field was a bog lake and the mound an island. The island was called 'Inis na mBeo' (The island of the living) and the lake was known as Lough Cré. In 1140 the Augustinians took over the older settlement and erected the current church on the site and planted the beech trees that tower over the ruins today. There are many legends connected with the former lake and its island. One tells us that no woman could ever set foot in the water or cross it without dying instantly. Another legend claims that it was impossible to die while on the island. Enough good reasons to build a monastery there. The Augustinians left the site in 1485 and the lake and surrounding bog was drained in 18th and 19th centuries to make the land suitable for farming.

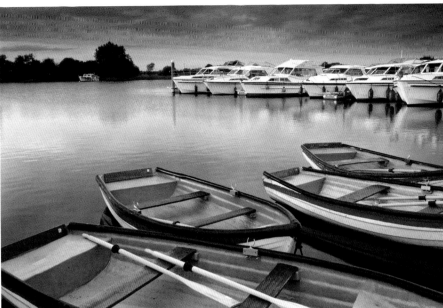

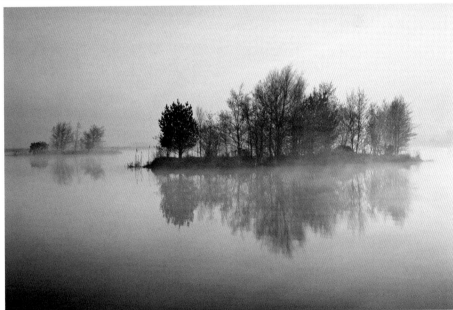

Left page: Monaincha Abbey, Co. Tipperary
Right page top: Boats at Banagher Harbour, Co. Offaly
Right page bottom: Lough Clochán, Boora Parklands, Co. Offaly

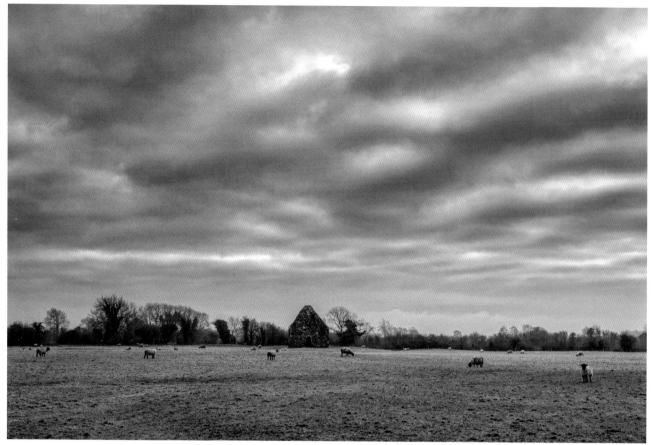

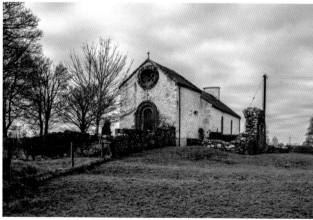

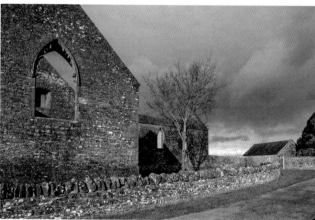

Left page top: Rahan Churches, Co. Offaly
Left page bottom left: Church of St Carthage, Rahan Churches, Co. Offaly
Left page bottom right: Aghaboe Abbey, Co. Laois
Right page: St Canice's Church, Aghaboe, Co. Laois

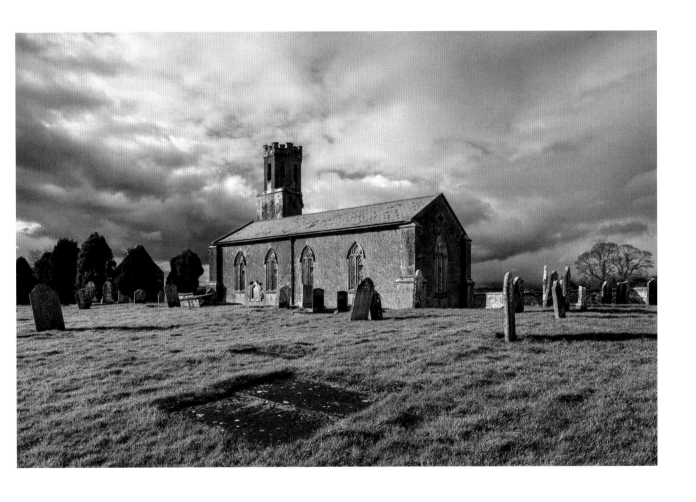

Aghaboe Abbey looks back on a long and tortured history. It was founded around 576AD by St Canice, plundered and destroyed by the Vikings in 913AD, rebuilt in 1052 only to be burned to the ground again in 1116. It was rebuilt again in 1189 and destroyed once again in 1346 as a casualty of an attack on the Norman castle that stood in an adjoining field. Another rebuild happened in 1382 and after that Aghaboe experienced some peace before Henry VIII put an end to the monasteries in Ireland in the 16th century.

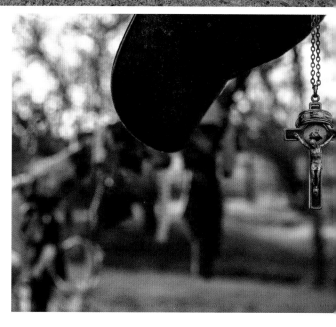

Left page top: St Anthony's Well and Mass Rock, Co. Offaly
Left page bottom: Seven Holy Wells, Killeigh, Co. Offaly
Right page: St Cieran's Bush, Co. Offaly

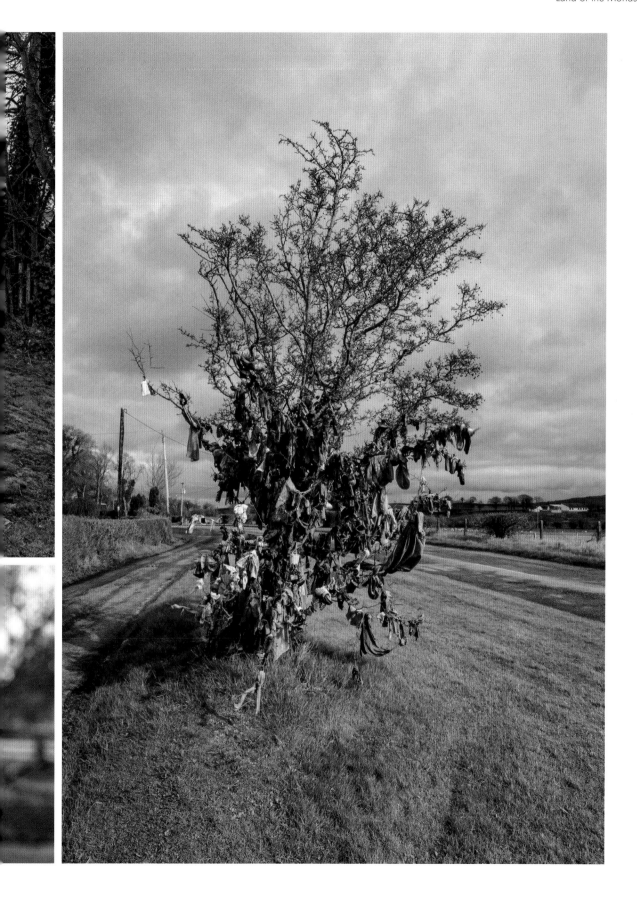

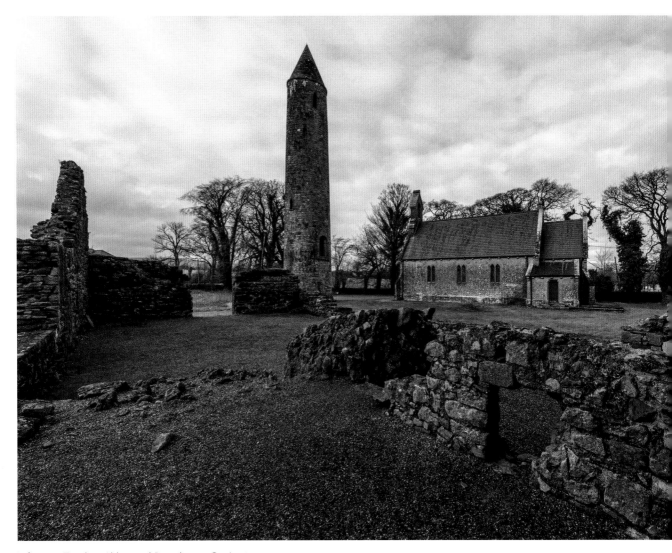

Left page: Timahoe Abbey and Roundtower, Co. Laois
Right page: St Mochua's Desk, Timahoe, Co. Laois

The story of Timahoe (from the Irish 'Teach Mochua', 'Mochua's House') begins in the 7th century when Mochua, a soldier from Connaught converted to the Christian faith at the age of 30. According to legend he retreated from the world and lived his live as a hermit and only had a rooster, a mouse and a fly as company. The rooster reminded him of the prayer times, the mouse made sure he never slept more than three hours and the fly would mark his position in the psalter. A similar story exists about Colman MacDuagh, another hermit monk who lived in a cave in the Burren of Co. Clare.

A monastic community existed in Timahoe up to 1650. The oldest remaining structure from the original monastery is the round tower which dates from the 12th century. In 2004 sculptor Michael Burke created St Mochua's Desk, a sculpture that features the psalter, the rooster, the mouse and the fly and which stands in the church grounds close to the round tower.

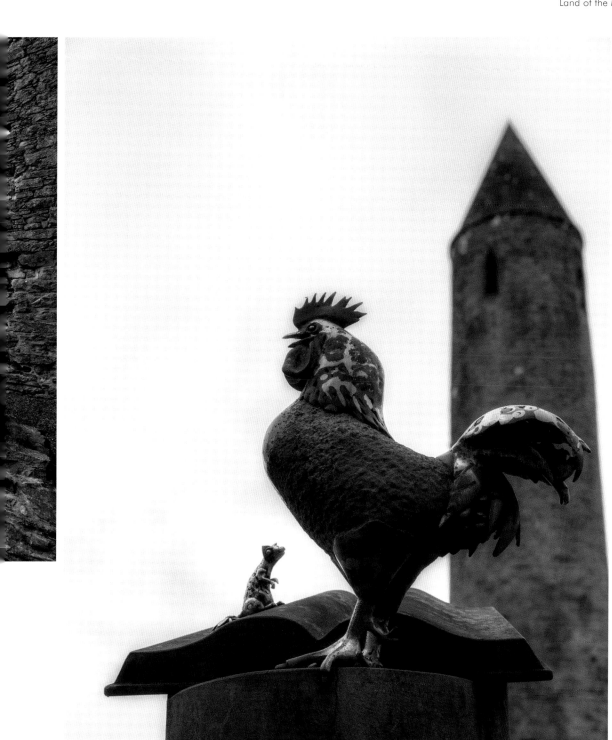

Left page top: Straw Bales, Co. Kildare
Left page bottom left: Roadside Poppies, Co. Kildare
Left page bottom right: St Brigid's Well, Co. Kildare
Right page: St Brigid's Cathedral Church, Co. Kildare

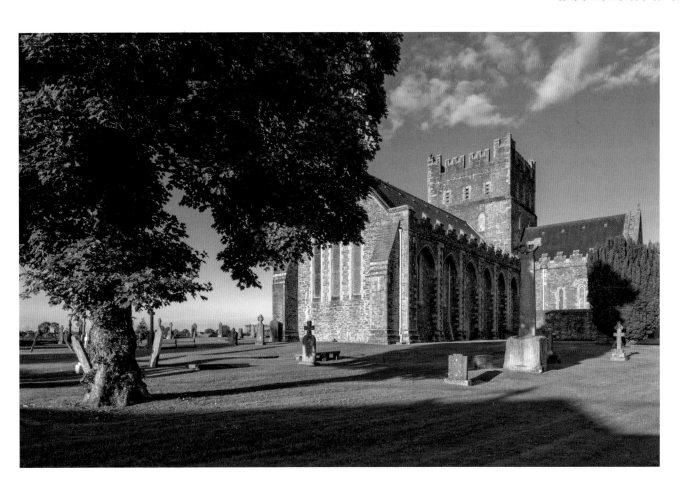

The cathedral in Kildare ('The Church of the Oak') town holds a special place in Irish Christian history. St Brigid who would became one of Ireland's patron saints arrived in Kildare together with her seven companions in 480AD. She established a nunnery and soon after also a friary and school of art. After Brigid's death around 525AD all institutions including the friary remained under the rule of the abbess and even the bishop was subordinate in jurisdiction to the abbess.

The building that occupies the site today is a restored Norman cathedral dating from 1223. It is thought that the building stands in the same spot that has been the site of a shrine to the pagan goddess Brigid and later of the church of St Brigid.

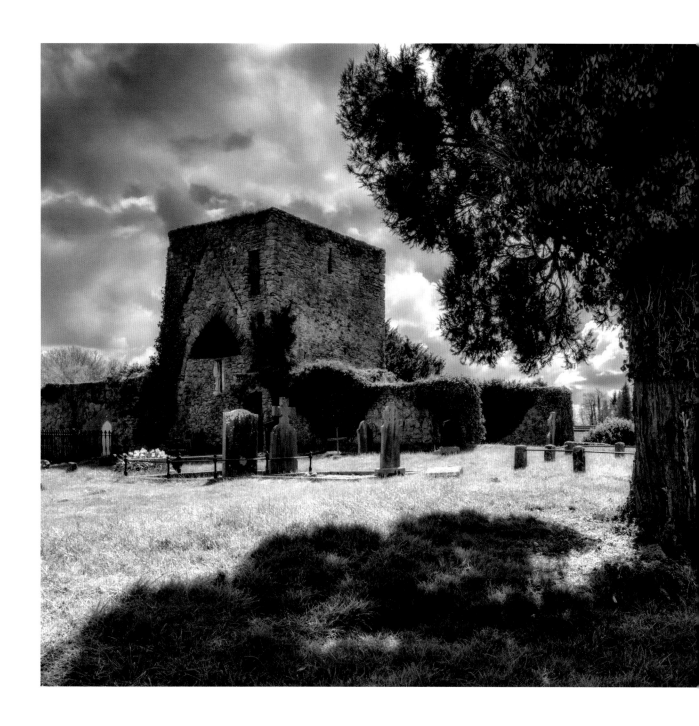

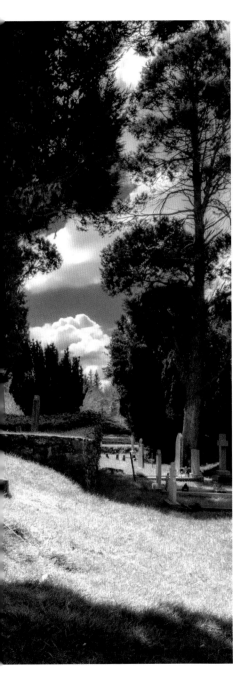

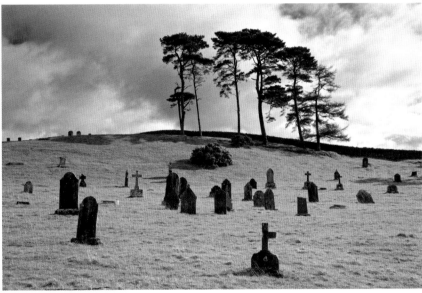

Left page: Black Abbey, Co. Kildare
Right page: Curragh Graveyard, Co. Kildare

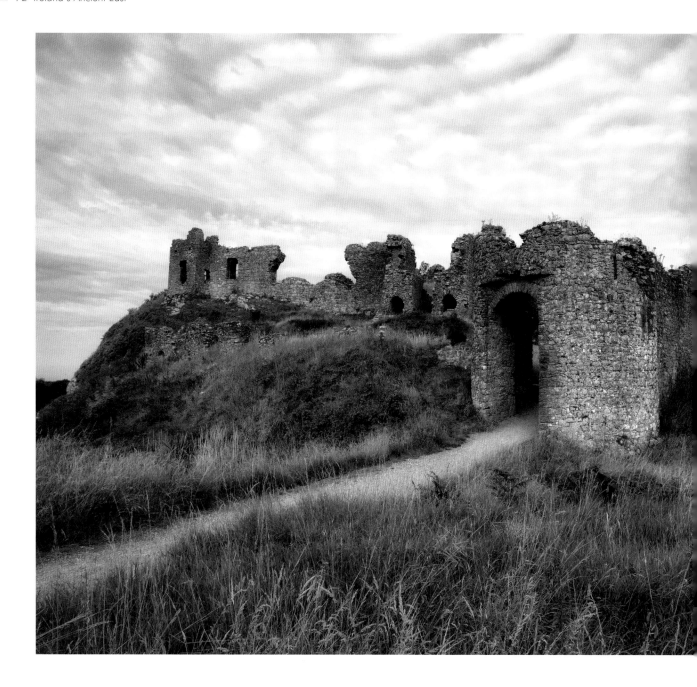

CASTLES AND CONQUESTS

The Rock of Dunamese and its castle ruins dominate the landscape of Co. Laois. The first settlement on this rocky outcrop has been dated to the 9th century when an early Christian hill fort, Dun Masc, was constructed on the rock, of which some remains of the outer wall survive to this day.

It is not entirely clear who built the Anglo-Norman castle; Meilyr FitzHenry and William Marshal are, however, the most likely candidates. Construction begun in the late 12th century and an impressive fortification that used the natural defence features of the rock was erected. The complex contained at least four lines of defence, an outer and inner barbican, a curtain wall and a massive keep.

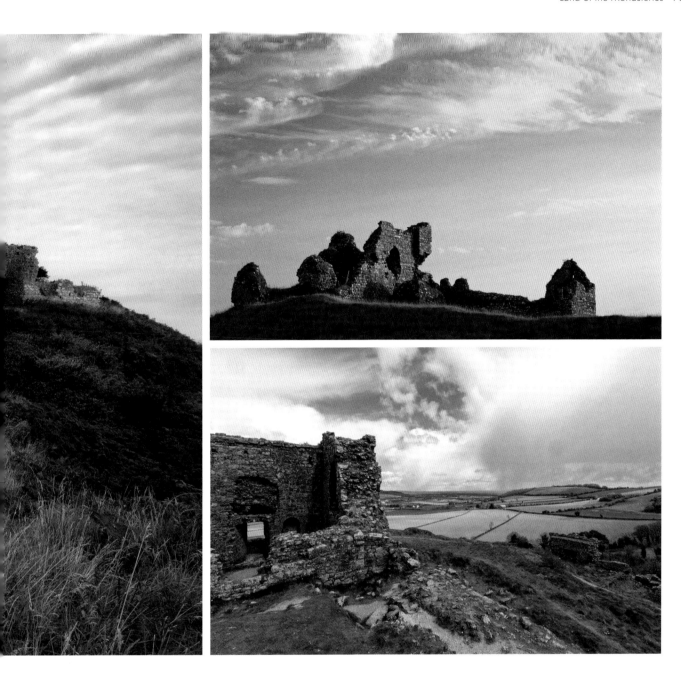

The castle at Clonmacnoise dates from the early 1200s and was built by the Anglo Normans to control the important crossing point at the river Shannon; it's thought to have been abandoned in the 1300s during an Irish uprising.

Left page: Rock of Dunamese, Co. Laois
Right page top: Clonmacnoise Castle, Co. Offaly
Right page bottom: Rock of Dunamese, Co. Laois

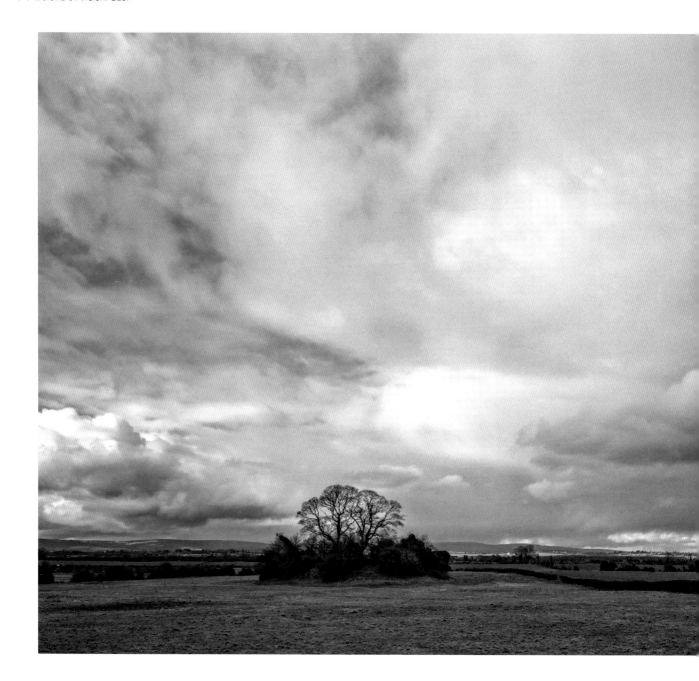

The Slieve Blooms are a gentle mountain range that rise from Ireland's central plain and connect the counties of Offaly and Laois. Although today they only rise to a modest height of just over 500 metres, the Slieve Bloom Mountains are among the oldest mountain ranges in Europe and once they reached almost 4000 meters.

The lower slopes are covered in forest, further up bog and heath take over. The peaks of the Slieve Blooms are separated by picturesque river valleys and can be explored by an extensive network of signposted trails.

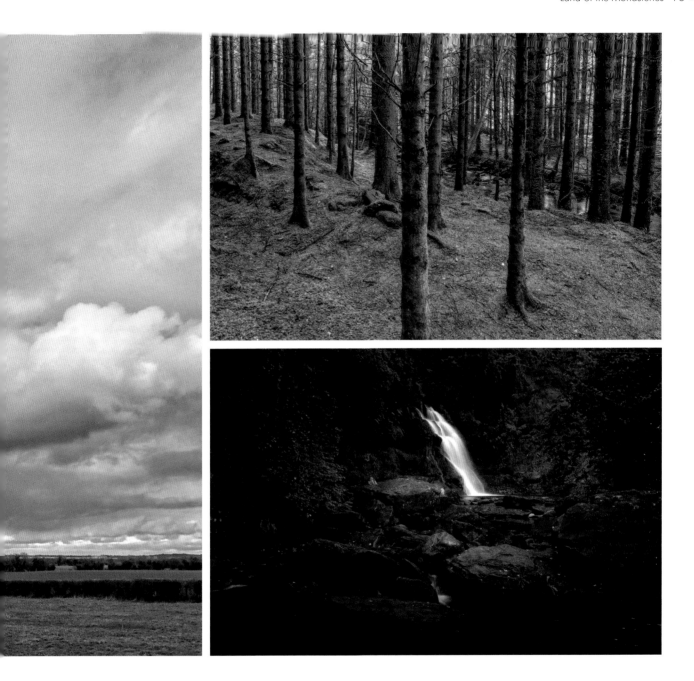

Left page: Aghaboe Motte, Co. Laois
Right page top: Glenbarrow, Co. Laois
Right page bottom: Clamp Hole Waterfall, Glenbarrow, Co. Laois

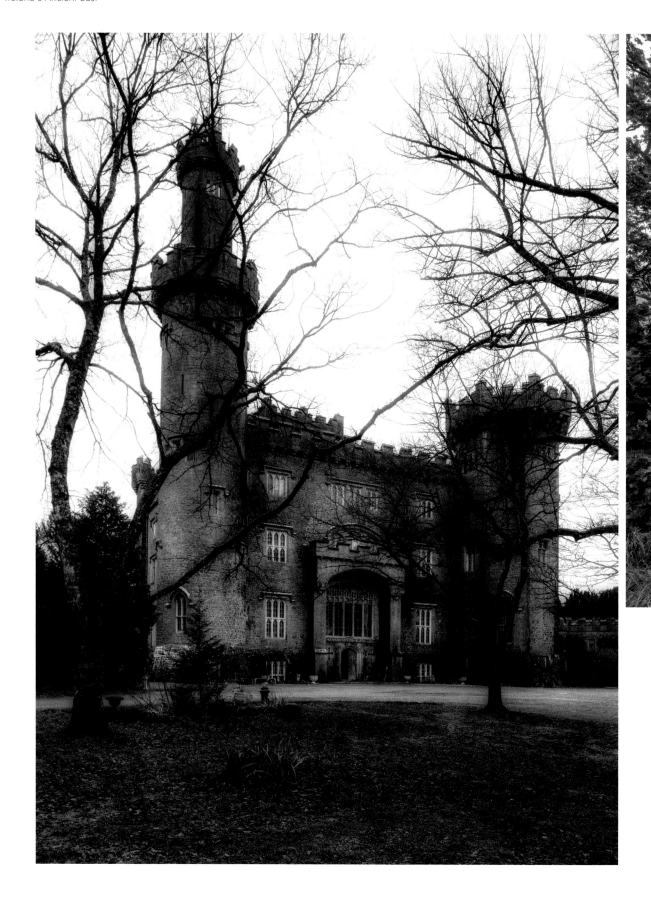

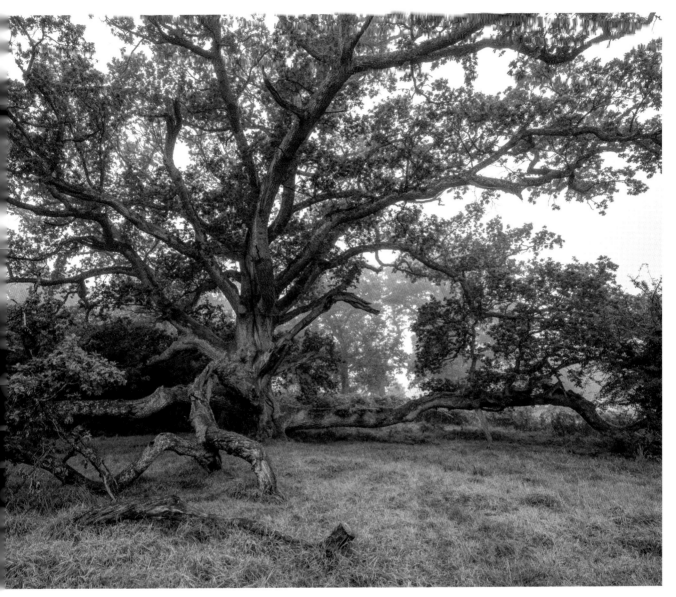

Left page: Charleville Castle, Tullamore, Co. Offaly
Right page: The King Oak, Charleville Estate, Tullamore, Co. Offaly

BIG HOUSES AND HARD TIMES

The King Oak stands on the grounds of the Charleville Estate outside Tullamore. This old sentinel with its gravity defying branches is tightly connected with the Hutton-Bury family, the owners of the estate. It is said that whenever a branch falls from the tree a member of the family will die. In 1963 a bolt of lightning struck the oak and indeed legend came true: Colonel Charles Hutton-Bury passed away a few weeks later.

Further up the roadway stands the home of the Hutton-Bury family, Charleville Castle, a gothic dream made reality by Charles William Bury, Earl of Charleville, and architect Francis Johnston, who also designed the GPO in Dublin. The current building replaced an older mansion house and was finished in 1812. Due to the often lavish lifestyle and resulting lack of resources of the owners, Charleville Castle remained unoccupied at times and was abandoned for good in 1912. Today the castle is in the hands of the Charleville Castle Heritage Trust, a group of volunteers who brought the building back from the brink of decay and restored much of its former glory and magic.

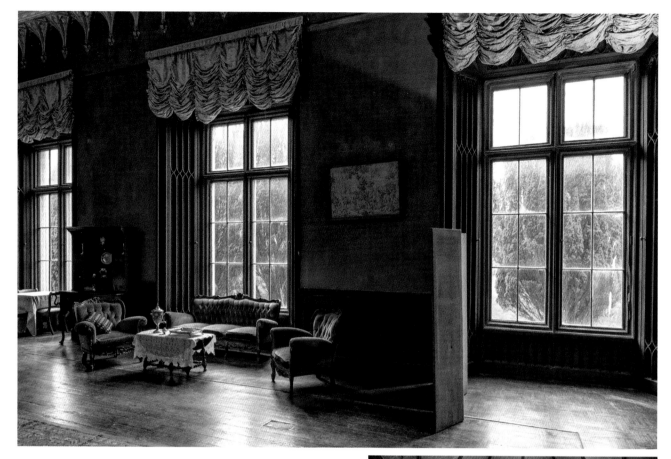

Left page top: Lounge, Charleville Castle, Tullamore, Co. Offaly
Left page bottom: Library, Charleville Castle, Tullamore, Co. Offaly
Right page: Harriet's Stairs, Charleville Castle, Tullamore, Co. Offaly

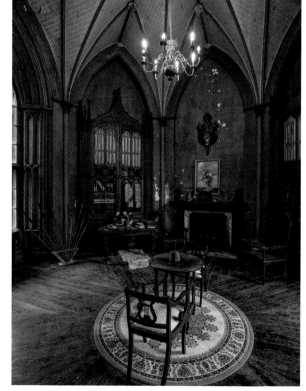

One of the most captivating places inside the castle is the main staircase, today known as Harriet's Stairs. Harriet, youngest daughter of the 3rd Earl of Charleville, died tragically when she fell down the staircase, aged just eight, in April 1861. Her singing, laughter and screaming can still be heard in the middle of the night and has been reported many times by different people. Some believe they have seen the image of a blonde girl in a blue and white dress.

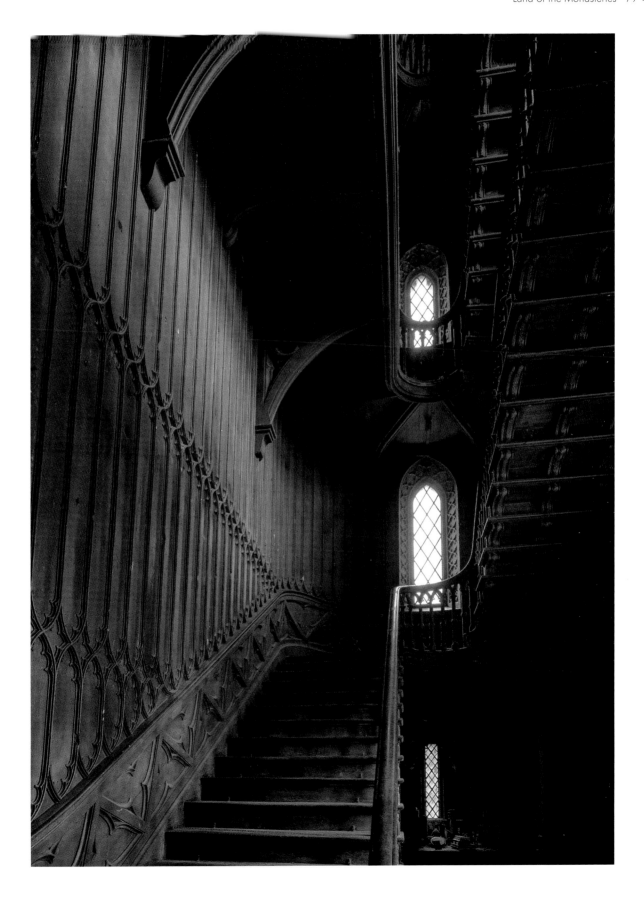

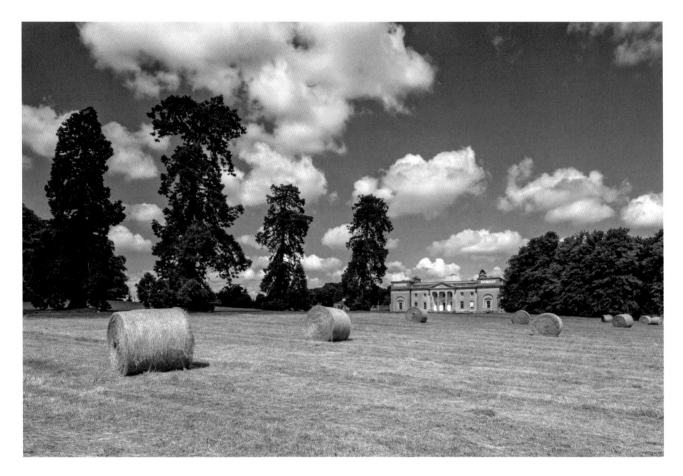

Left page: Emo Court, Co. Laois
Right page top: Castletown House, Co. Kildare
Right page bottom: Castletown House Facade, Co. Kildare

Emo Court is a neo-classical mansion near the village of Emo in Co. Laois and it took an unusually long time – 70 years – to build. James Gandon, designer of the Customs House in Dublin, did the designs and John Dawson, 1st Earl of Portarlington, started work on the house in 1790. But Irish history intervened; the 1st Earl died during the 1798 Rebellion, the 2nd Earl developed the interiors and gardens in the 1830s until the Great Famine in the 1840s brought the work to a halt again. Henry, 3rd Earl of Portarlington, eventually finished the building work in 1860 and Emo Court experienced forty years of splendour.

The outbreak of World War One in 1914 and the Easter Rising in 1916 and subsequent War of Independence in Ireland made the Earls of Portarlington, like many other Protestant landowners, leave for England. Emo Court lay abandoned for many decades. In 1930 Emo Court was sold to the Jesuits and one of its first new inhabitants was Father Francis Brown, famed for his photographs of Irish landscapes and people. Later Major Cholmley-Harrison bought and restored the building; in 1994 he handed it over to the people of Ireland, though he continued to live there until his death in 2008

and is today memorialised by a cherry blossom tree in the gardens. Emo Court is now managed by the Office of Public Works (OPW) and visitors can take guided tours of the house or walk in the gardens.

Castletown House is Ireland's oldest and largest Palladian-style house and was built on an impressive estate between 1722 and 1729 for William Connolly, Speaker of the Irish House of Commons, and one of the wealthiest men in Ireland at the time. The facade was designed by Italian architect Alessandro Galilei, the wings by Irish architect Sir Edward Lovett Pearce. Guided tours of the house are available where visitors can admire the beautiful galleries and internal plasterwork, or tour the gardens.

This I believe the only house in Ireland to which the term palace can be applied.

Richard Twiss, 1775

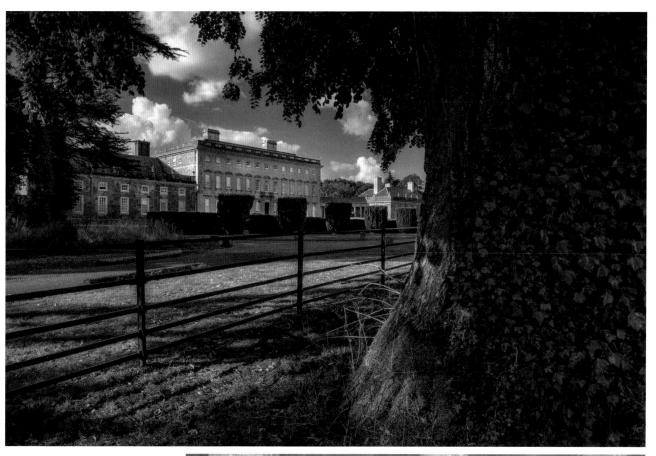

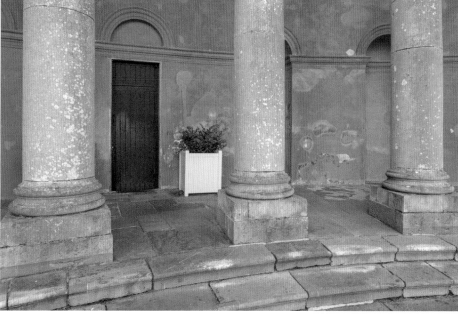

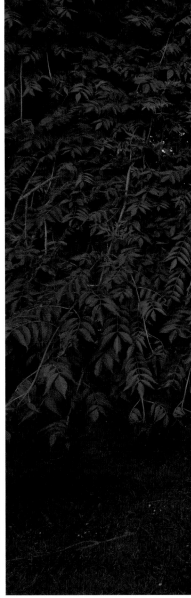

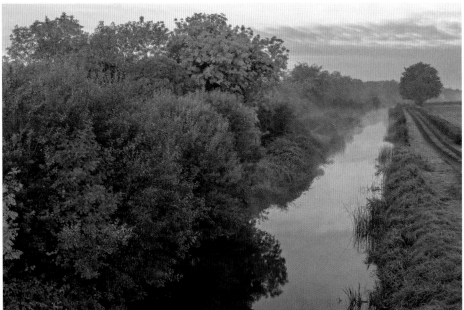

The Royal and the Grand Canals were both built in the 18th century to connect the river Liffey in Dublin with Ireland's main waterway the river Shannon. While the construction of the Grand Canal had to overcome a number of obstacles, mainly how to successfully build a canal through the Bog of Allen, a rival company started work on the Royal Canal further north.

Both canals opened in 1817. By the 1830s the Royal Canal carried 80,000 tonnes of freight and 40,000 passengers a year. By the end of the 19th century the railway network gradually eroded the business on both canals and they started to fall into disuse and eventually disrepair. In 1999 Waterways Ireland assumed responsibility for the Grand and the Royal Canal and both are used today for recreation and pleasure.

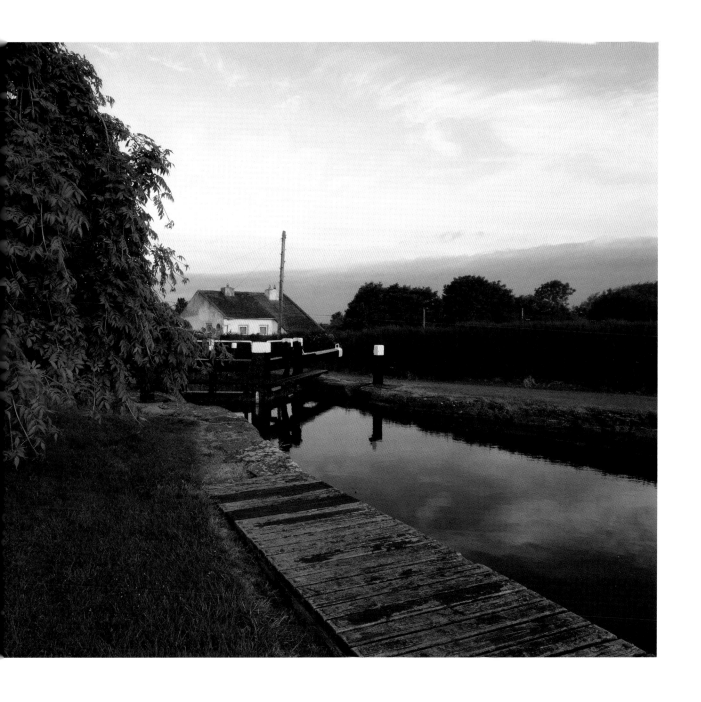

Left page: Royal Canal, Hill of Down, Co. Meath
Right page: Grand Canal, Rathangan, Co. Kildare

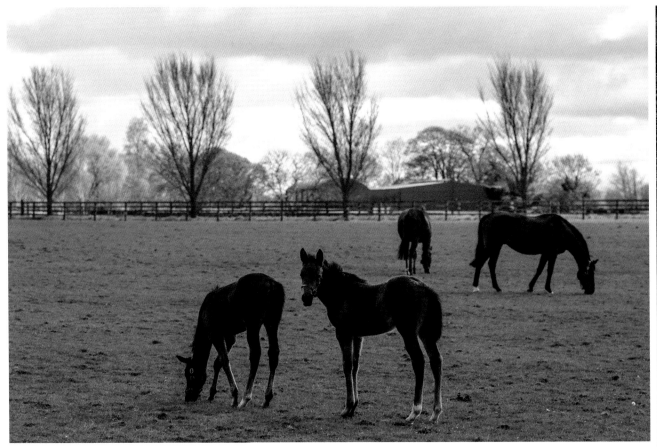

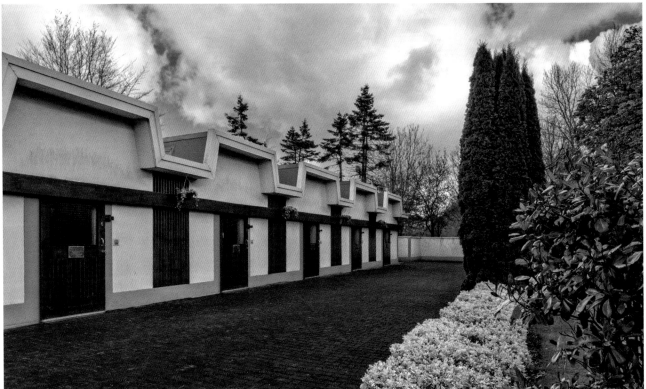

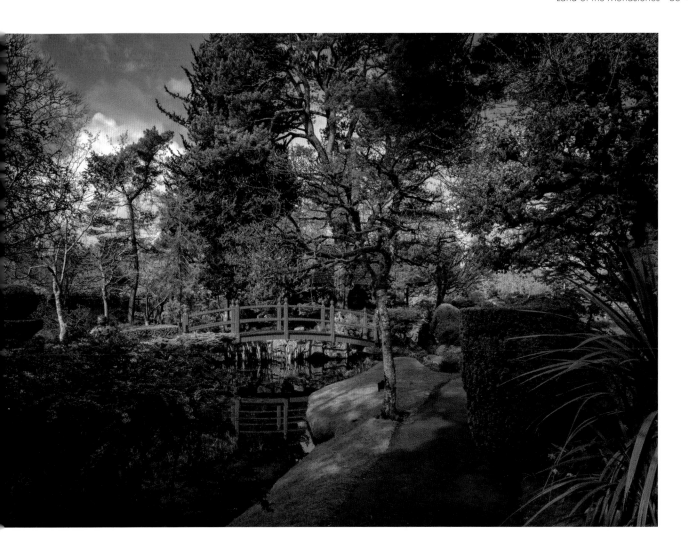

Left page top: Foals, The National Stud, Co. Kildare
Left page bottom: Stallion Boxes, The National Stud, Co. Kildare
Right page: Japanese Gardens, The National Stud, Co. Kildare

THE SPORT OF KINGS

The Curragh is one of Europe's oldest grasslands covering some twenty square kilometres. The name, which means 'place of running horses', gives a clear hint to the history of this flat open plain. Horse racing on the Curragh goes back to pre-Christian times, back to the time of legend; the nearby Hill of Allen was the meeting place of the Fianna and this mythical band of warriors were the first ones to run their horses on this plain. In the third century it is said kings and chieftains raced their chariots on the Curragh, it is likely that in the seventeenth century members of the aristocracy held private race meetings and the first recorded race took place in 1772. The tradition is still alive and the Curragh is synonymous with horse racing: The Curragh racecourse is one of the best known in Ireland and the nearby National Stud has bred and trained numerous champion horses.

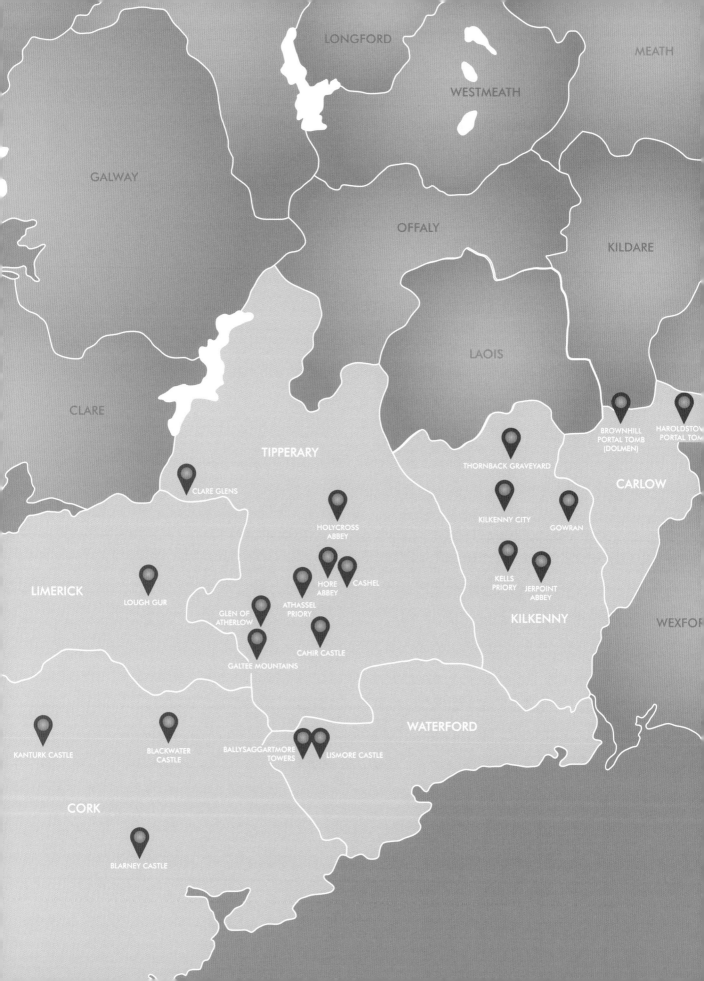

LAND OF THE RIVER VALLEYS

ANCIENT IRELAND

Lough Gur is a horseshoe-shaped lake in County Limerick surrounded by gentle hills, fields and hedgerows, but the area has a very special history. Excavations have shown that Lough Gur was one of the first Neolithic farming settlements in Ireland. The dwellings at the time were very similar to what we see today among African tribes: a round or rectangular structure with walls made of wood, hay and mud, topped by a thatched roof. The visitor centre at the eastern end of the lake is built in that style, but from more modern materials. The first humans arrived at Lough Gur around 3500BC and the place has been inhabited and farmed ever since. It all came to light when parts of the lake, which at the time completely surrounded what is now the peninsula of Knockadoon, were drained during the 1840s and pieces of pottery, flints, stone axes and spearheads and a bronze shield appeared. Archaeologists then started to explore the area in detail and discovered structures and artefacts from the early Stone Age, Bronze Age and Iron Age. These findings, together with the already known heritage from the middle ages and beyond, made Lough Gur one of the most important historic sites in Ireland.

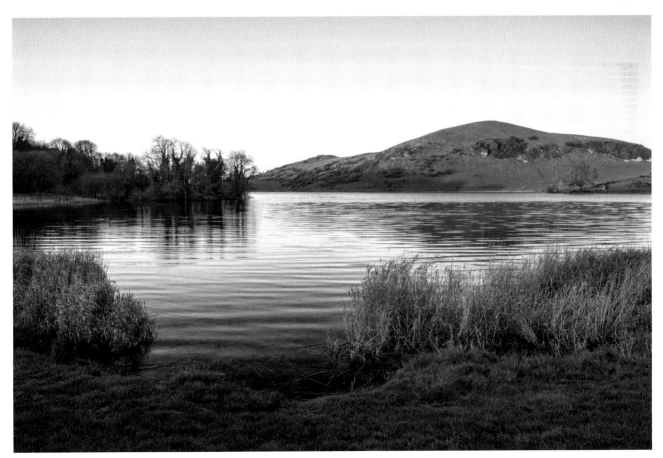

Eastern Shore of Lough Gur, Co. Limerick

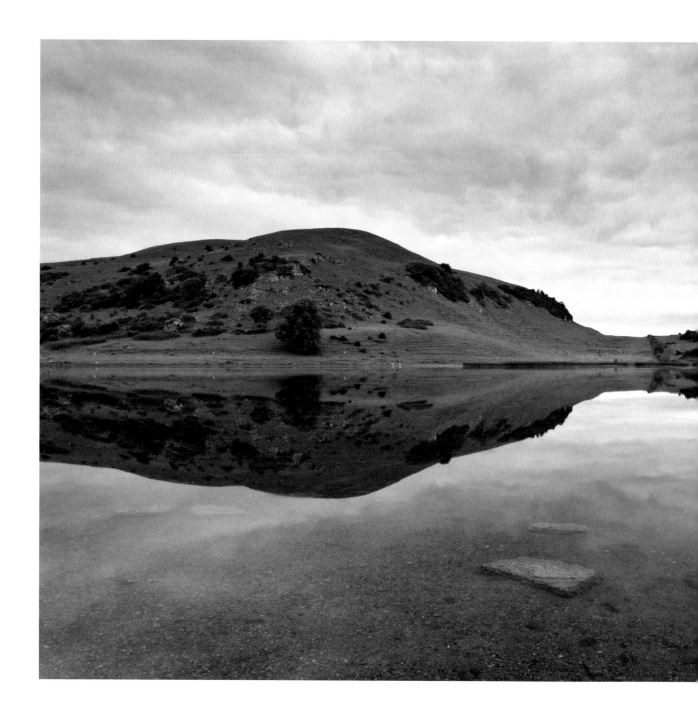

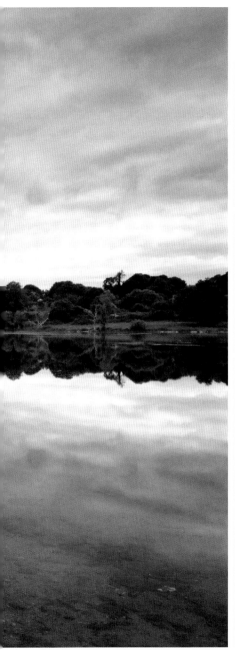

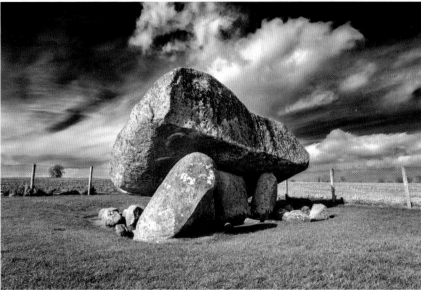

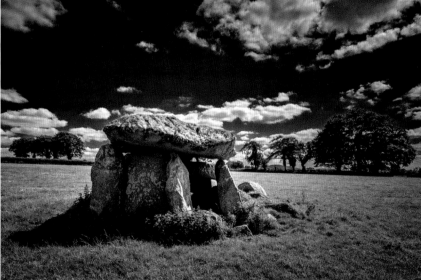

Left page: Summer Reflections, Lough Gur, Co. Limerick
Right page top: Browne's Hill Dolmen, Co. Carlow
Right page bottom: Haroldstown Portal Tomb, Co. Carlow

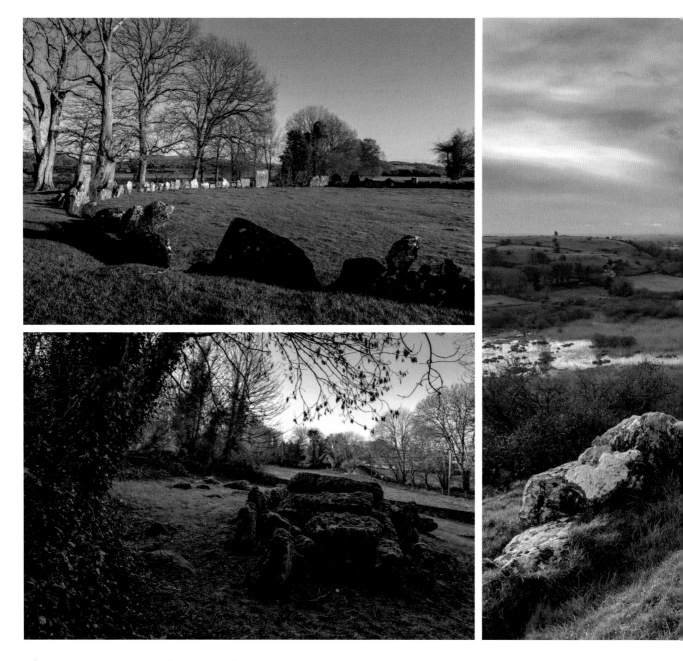

Left page top: Grange Stone Circle, Co. Limerick
Left page bottom: The Giant's Grave, Lough Gur, Co. Limerick

At the western end of Lough Gur stands the impressive Grange Stone Circle, the largest stone circle in Ireland. When the sun rises on the summer solstice, the sunlight passes directly between the entrance stones and lights up the centre of the circle. It's thought to have been used in rituals; excavations uncovered numerous pieces of pottery that seemed to have been deliberately smashed, human and animal bones and some bronze materials have been found. Grange Stone Circle is 45 metres in diameter, enclosed by 113 standing stones and an embankment. The largest of the stones, named after the pagan god Crom Cruach, is 4 metres tall and weighs some 4 tonnes. To the north of the stone circle is another smaller circle and a solitary standing stone.

The Giant's Grave, as it is known locally, is a wedge tomb dating from 2500BC. Its more recent history was quite colourful, as a newspaper report from 1833 shows: 'An old woman resided in it for many years and on her death the covering stones were thrown off and it was left in its present state by money diggers who only found some burned bones in an old jug that surely was not worth one brass farthing.'

During excavations in 1938 the remains of at least eight adults and four children were found below the stone slabs. Close to the tomb the entire and intact skeleton of an ox – thought to have been a sacrificial offering to the gods – was discovered.

There are a number of enclosures and ringforts at Lough Gur and the

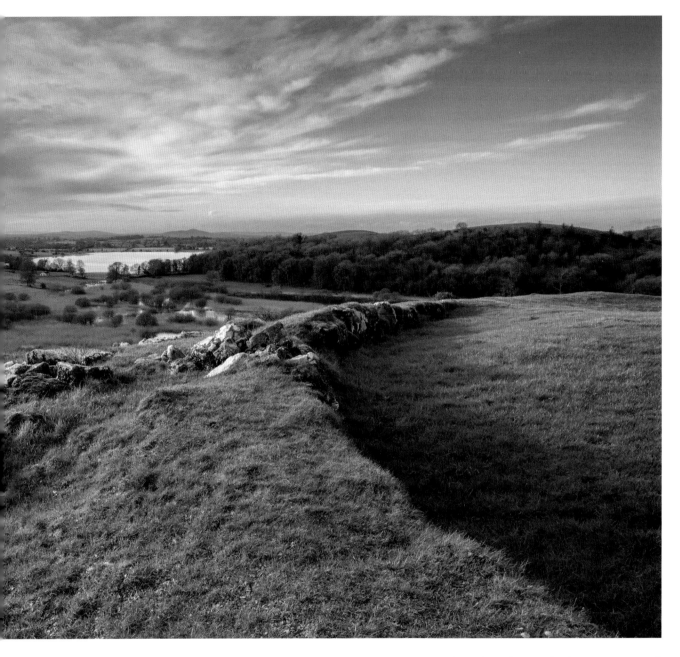

Right page: Carraig Aille Ringfort with Lough Gur in the distance, Co. Limerick

surrounding hills. These enclosures and ringforts were the first fortified farms in Ireland: one or more huts were surrounded by a circular wall made of stone or dirt. In the case of an attack people and livestock could take shelter within the enclosure. These forts varied massively in size: some were built to shelter a single family, others were big enough to host an entire community. The oldest, dating from the Neolithic era, are located at Knockadoon. Two impressive Iron Age ringforts (from around the 10th century) sit on top of Carraig Aille overlooking the lake and provide panoramic views over the countryside of Co. Limerick and Tipperary. Just beside the Lough Gur Visitor Centre at the eastern side of the lake are *The Spectacles*, the remains of an early medieval farm

consisting of field boundary walls and hut sites.

Later the principal design of the ringfort was adjusted to create a new kind of homestead: the crannóg. Crannógs are artificial islands built in lakes and sometimes rivers. The earliest examples date from the Neolithic but it is thought that most crannogs were built during the bronze and Iron Age. Lough Gur alone had at least 3 crannógs, Ireland in total has an estimated 1,200 examples and many of them have been discovered more or less by chance during underwater surveys. Some could only be reached by boat, others had a slightly submerged causeway.

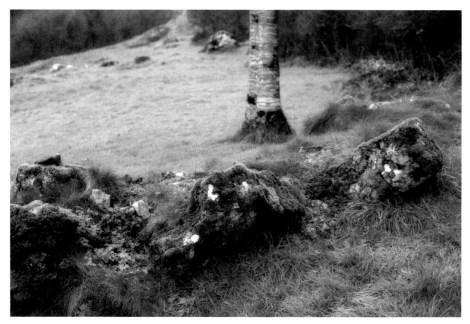

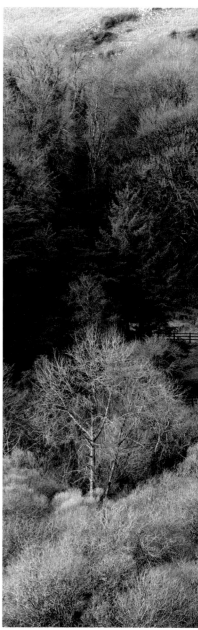

Bouchier's Castle protects the eastern entrance to Knockadoon; its typical tower-house structure dates from the early 1600s and was built for Sir George Bouchier, son of the second Earl of Bath. The lands around Lough Gur were granted to Bouchier after the fall of the Earls of Desmond who had ruled over the province of Munster before. Bouchier's Castle stands at the exact spot of an older Earls of Desmond stronghold and some features of the older structure have been incorporated into it. Legend has it, however, that the Earls of Desmond never really disappeared from the area; it's said that every seven years Gerald Fitzgerald, 3rd Earl of Desmond (a chief justice of Ireland and poet) rides his silver-shod white horse out of and around the lake.

Geároid lives there in the under-lake world to this day, awaiting the time of his normal return to the world of men. But once in every seven years, on clear moonlight nights, he emerges temporarily, when the Lough Gur peasantry sees him as a phantom mounted on a phantom white horse, leading a phantom or fairy cavalcade across the lake and land.

Evans-Wentz, W. Y., *The Fairy-faith in Celtic Countries*, London: H. Frowde, 1911

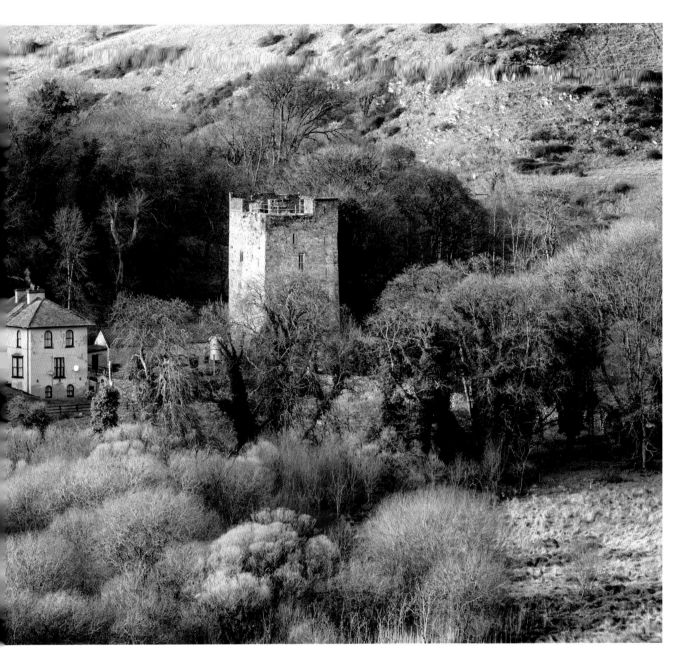

Left page: The Spectacles, Lough Gur, Co. Limerick
Right page: Bouchier's Castle, Lough Gur, Co. Limerick

Once he has managed to wear down his horse's silver shoes, Gerald will regain mortal form again and restore the glory of the Desmonds. Another tower house known as the Black Castle, now in ruins, guards the western approaches of Knockadoon.

Other legends tell of a town existing like a miniature Atlantis under the waters of Lough Gur. When you are out on the lake on a calm day, when the lake is motionless, it is said you can see the houses, walls and castles under the surface of the water. The French engineer Charles Vallancey wrote in 1812: 'It astonished me to see such immense irregular blocks and rocks under water, when nothing similar is to be found in the vicinity.'

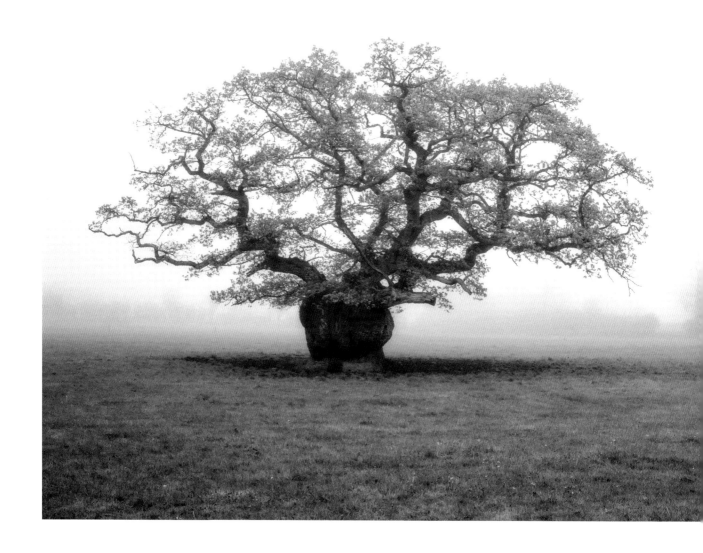

Left page: Oak, Harley Park, Co. Tipperary
Right page top: Teampall Nua, Lough Gur, Co. Limerick
Right page bottom: Sunset near Cashel, Co. Tipperary

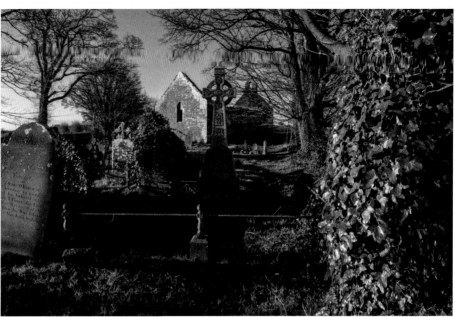

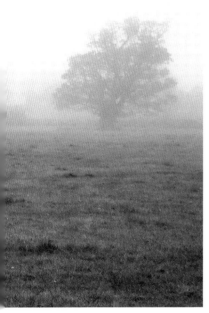

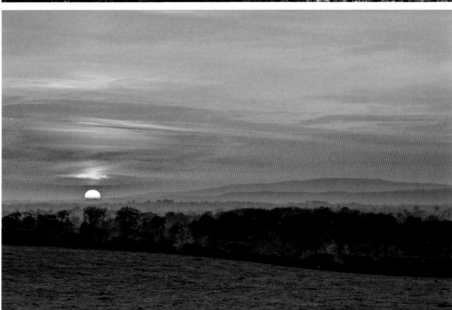

SACRED IRELAND

By Lough Gur's romantic shore, Where the shamrock and the ivy ever grow; Where the wild dove and the raven like protecting spirits soar O'er the green graves of silent Teampall Nua.

Owen Bresnan

Below you lies the great Plain of Tipperary with the little white roads criss crossing through the greenness of fields and the darker green of woods. West of Cahir are the Galtee Mountains and on the east is Slievenamon. On a good day you can see the Rock of Cashel rising up from the green plain twenty miles to the north.

H.V. Morton, *In search of Ireland*

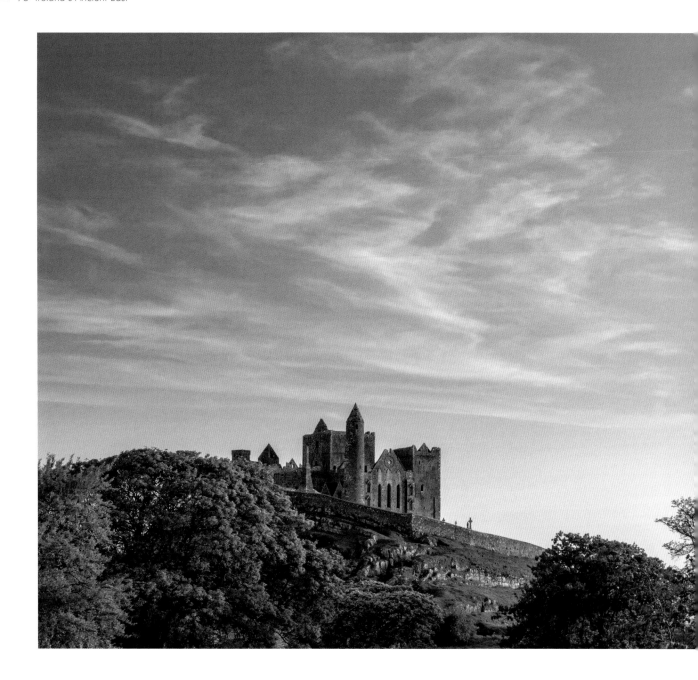

Left page: Rock of Cashel, Co. Tipperary
Right page: Cathedral and Round Tower, Rock of Cashel, Co. Tipperary

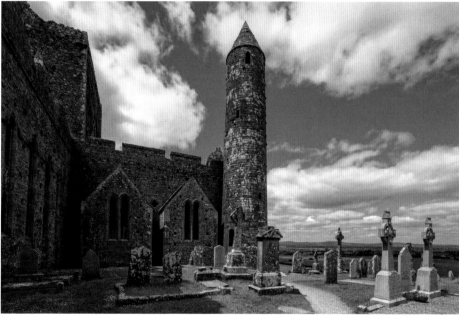

The Rock of Cashel is one of the most memorable landmarks in Ireland rising from the Golden Vale in Tipperary. According to legend the Rock came from a mountain some 30 kilometres north of Cashel: the Devil's Bit. As the story goes, the devil and Fionn MacCumhail, Ireland's legendary warrior, had a row and the devil, while chasing Fionn up the mountain, stubbed his big toe. This made the devil even angrier and in his rage he bit a piece of rock out of the mountain. Unfortunately for the devil, he broke all his teeth and the piece of rock fell out of his mouth where it stands today. In another, most likely Christianised, version the devil was fleeing from St Patrick when he took his bite from the mountain. The end result however was the same.

St Patrick's connection with the Rock of Cashel doesn't end here. The Rock of Cashel was the seat of the kings of Munster since the early 5th century and it is said that St. Patrick converted the pagan king of Munster Aengus MacMutfraich to Christianity at Cashel in 450AD. Although no signs remain today it is very likely that the Rock has been inhabited and fortified from very early on in history. Its Irish name, 'Ceiseal', means 'stone fort' and its location makes the Rock of Cashel the perfect place for a stronghold with much of County Tipperary visible in all directions making it impossible for an enemy to approach undetected.

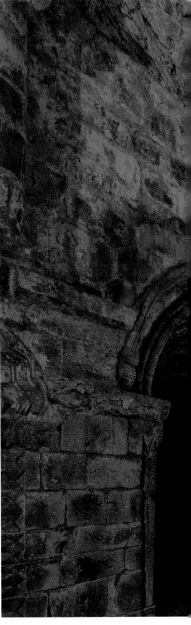

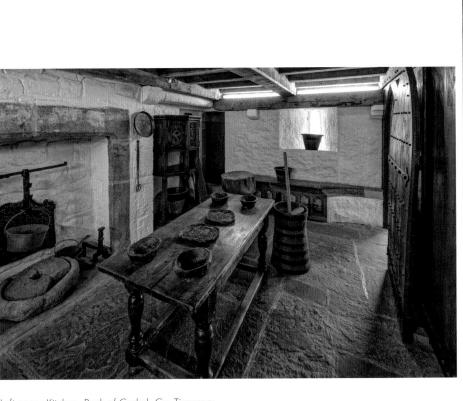

Left page: Kitchen, Rock of Cashel, Co. Tipperary
Right page: Cormac's Chapel, Rock of Cashel, Co. Tipperary

After Aengus's conversion to Christianity, Cashel remained the seat of the kings of Munster for several more centuries. During that time Cashel also became the seat of the first High King of Ireland, Brian Boru, who was the first to unify Ireland under one rule. Brian was crowned High King in 990AD and ruled for twenty-four years, until his death, defeating the Vikings at the Battle of Clontarf in 1014.

In 1101 Muirchertach O'Brien, king of Munster, self-proclaimed High King of Ireland and a great-grandson of Brian Boru, donated the Rock of Cashel to the Catholic Bishop of Limerick and only ten years later Cashel became the seat of one of only two archbishops in Ireland. The town of Cashel was founded sometime around 1218 and a Dominican priory was established in 1243. The oldest and, at 28 metres high, tallest surviving building on the rock, the round tower, was the first structure to be erected by the church. Cormac's Chapel, a Romanesque church, which forms a part of the cathedral today was built between 1127 and 1134 and features intricate architecture and some of the best-preserved

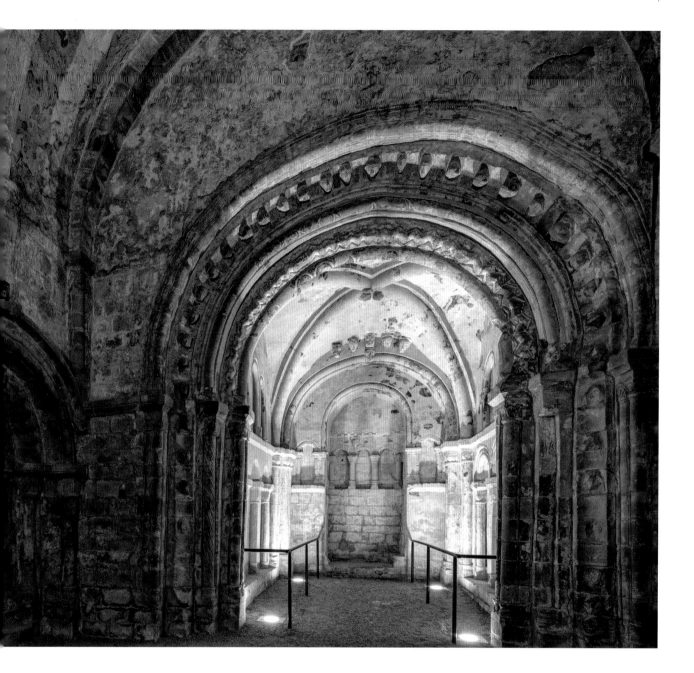

frescoes in Ireland. Between 1235 and 1270 St Patrick's Cathedral was built and the now roofless building together with the round tower still dominate the Rock of Cashel today.

Cashel kept its importance as a political as well as religious centre until Ireland fell under English rule and its prosperous existence came to a sudden halt on 12 September 1647. On this day Lord 'Murrough O'Brien' Inchiquin launched a merciless and bloody attack on behalf of the English Parliament. According to General Ludlow, the 2nd in command of the invasion, some 3,000 were slaughtered including women, children, priests and friars. The cathedral was used by the Church of Ireland until 1749 when the site was abandoned in favour of a new cathedral in the town. The roof of the old cathedral was removed and over the years the building fell into decay.

Today the Rock of Cashel is managed by the OPW and is open to the public.

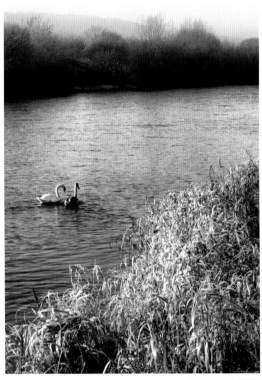

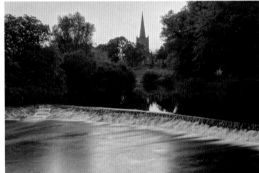

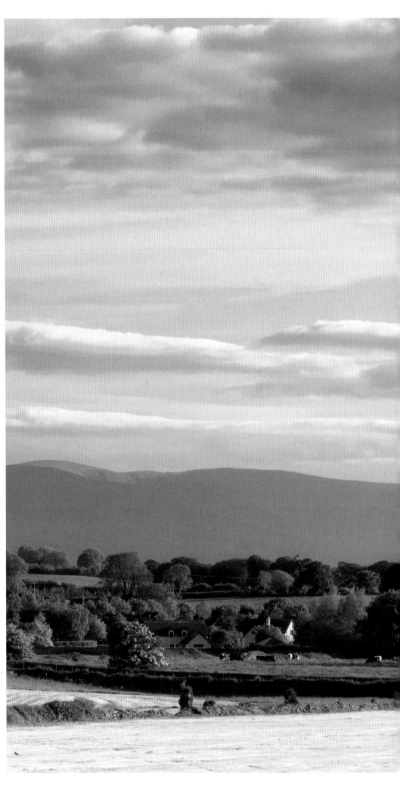

The River Suir rises at the slopes of the Devil's Bit Mountain in County Tipperary and winds its way over 185 kilometres to Waterford where it flows into the Atlantic Ocean. Along its way it passes villages and towns like Holycross, Golden, Cahir, Clonmel and Carrick-On-Suir, each steeped in history.

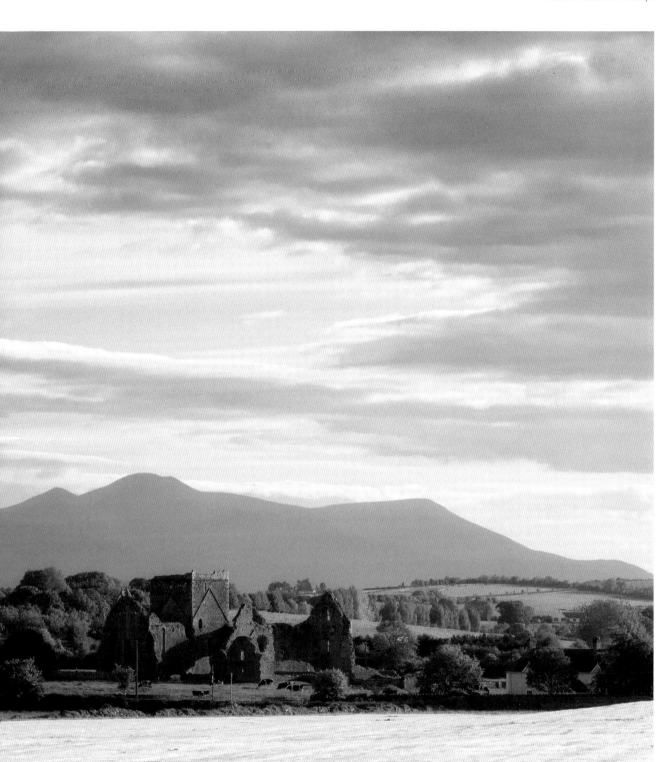

Left page top: Swans on the River Suir, Clonmel, Co. Tipperary
Left page bottom: River Suir, Cahir, Co. Tipperary
Right page: Hore Abbey, Cashel, Co. Tipperary

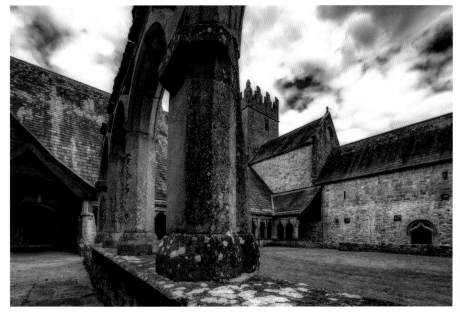

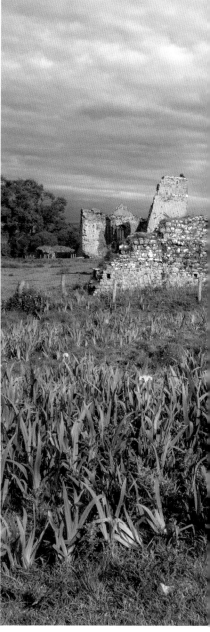

Holycross Abbey was a very popular pilgrim destination during the middle ages, because the it hosted a relic of the True Cross – the cross believed to be the one on which Jesus was crucified. It is said that Queen Isabella of Angouleme, widow of King John, bestowed the relic on the monastery.

In the 17th century, after the Cromwellian war, the abbey fell into ruins, but in 1969 special legislation enabled Holy Cross, which was labelled a National Monument at the time, to be restored and be used as a place of worship again which is exceptional for a National Monument.

Athassel Abbey near the village of Golden was founded for the Augustinian Order by William de Burgho in 1192. In the three centuries of its existence it grew into the largest priory in Ireland and a centre of spiritual and political importance. In its heyday the abbey was surrounded by a large town.

It survived one raid in 1329, but when the strong connection with the de Burgho family was broken in 1512 the abbey and town found themself in a steep decline. In 1552 Athassel Abbey was eventually abandoned by order of King Edward VI and in 1581 the abbey and remains of the town were plundered and burned.

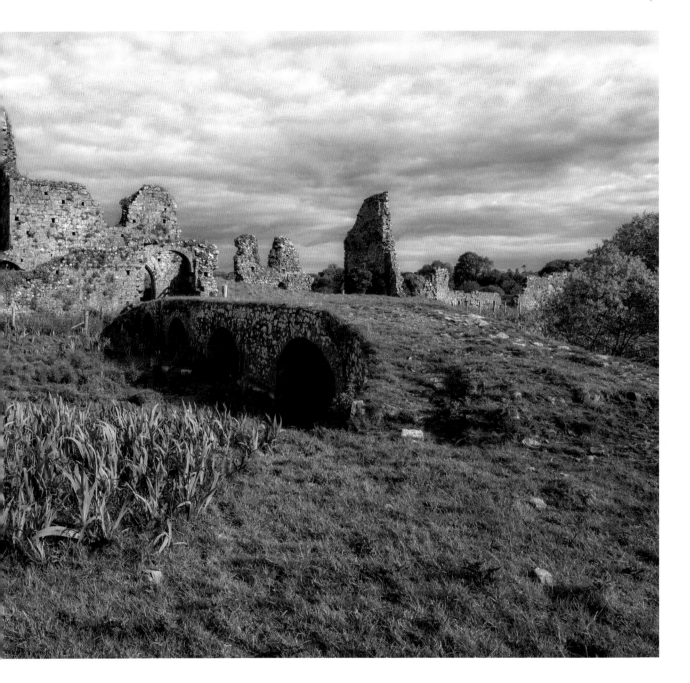

Left page: Holycross Abbey, Co. Tipperary
Right page: Athassel Abbey, Co. Tipperary

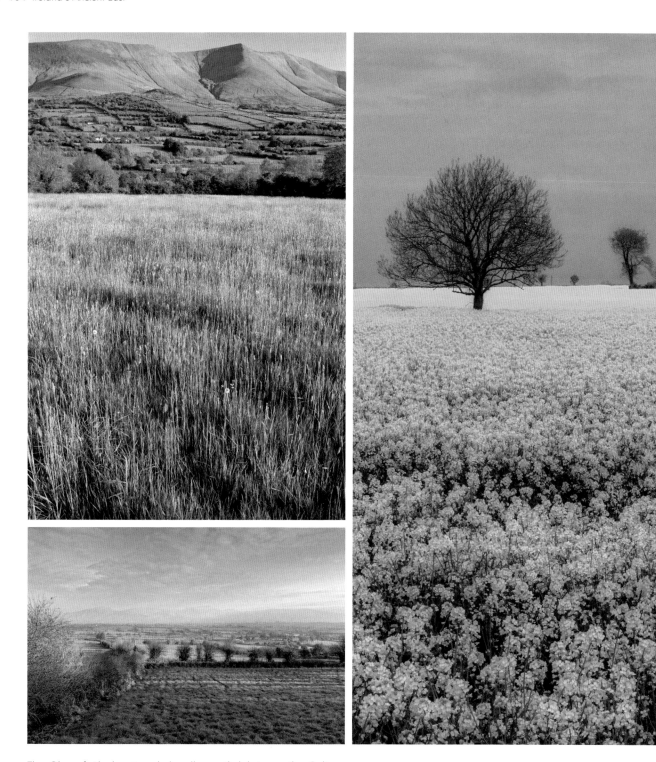

The Glen of Aherlow is a lush valley nestled between the Galtee Mountains, Ireland's highest inland mountain range, and the slopes of Slievenamuck. The valley is renowned for having been the refuge for Geoffrey Keating, a 17th-century historian and Tipperary native who had studied and obtained a doctorate in Bordeaux. Keating's major work Foras Feasa ar Eirinn (Foundation of Knowledge on Ireland) was completed in 1634, written in Irish and tells the story of Ireland from the creation to the arrival of the Normans.

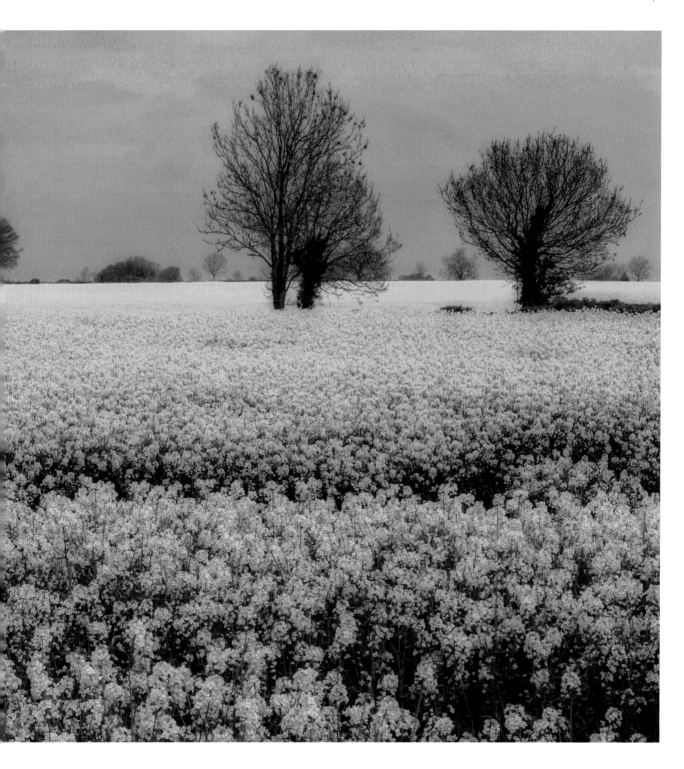

Left page top: Galtee Mountains, Glen of Aherlow, Co. Tipperary
Left page bottom: Galtee Mountains, Co. Tipperary
Right page: Rapeseed Field, Co. Tipperary

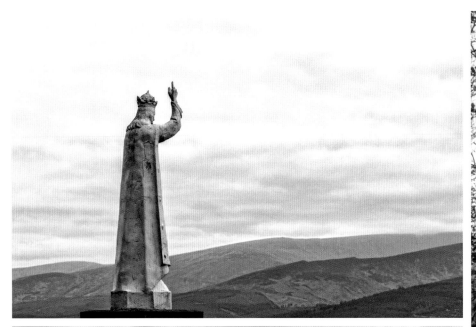

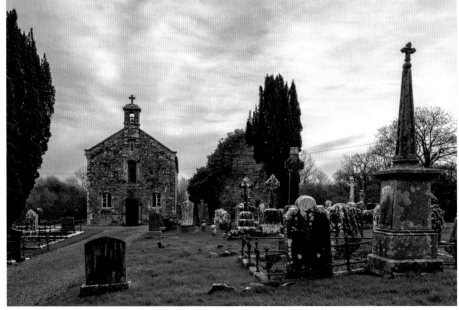

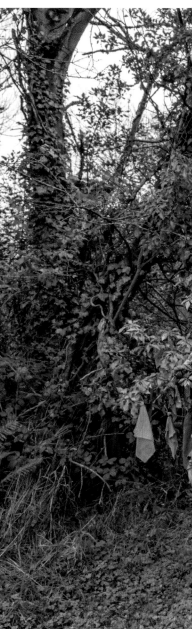

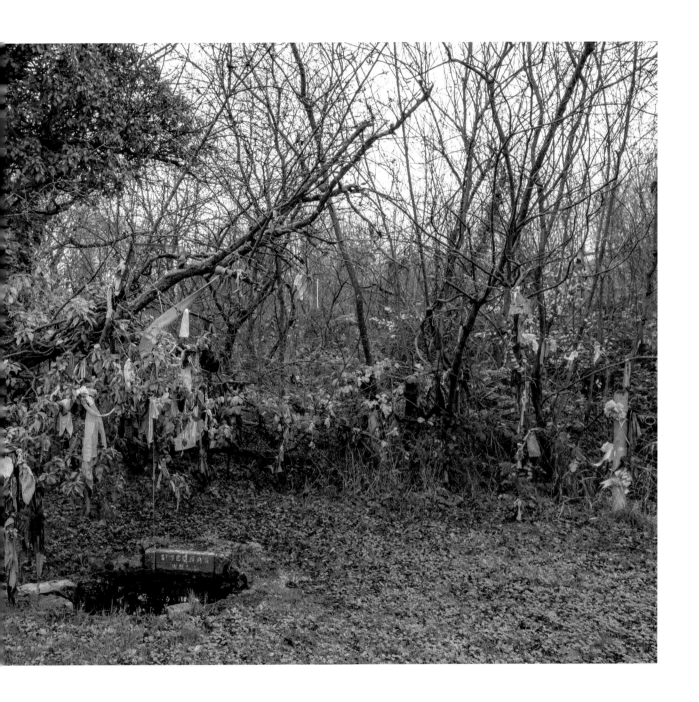

Left page top: Christ the King Statue, Glen of Aherlow, Co. Tipperary
Left page bottom: Clonbeg Church, Glen of Aherlow, Co. Tipperary
Right page: St Sedna's Well, Glen of Aherlow, Co. Tipperary

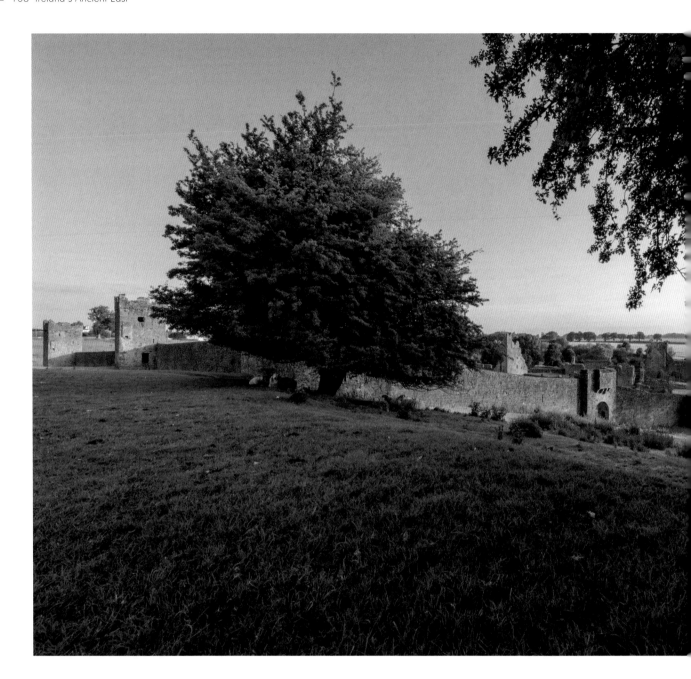

Left page: Kells Priory, Co. Kilkenny
Right page top: Thornback Cemetery, Co. Kilkenny
Right page bottom: Kilree Church and Roundtower, Co. Kilkenny

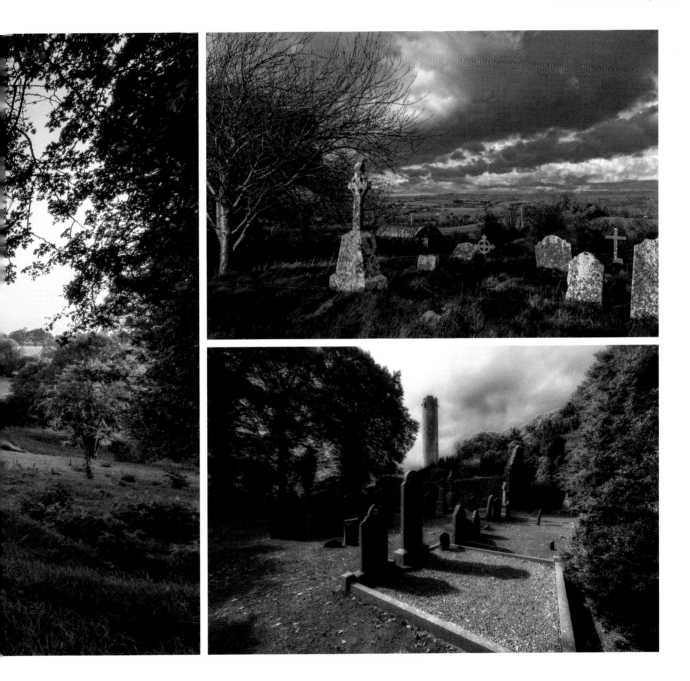

The Priory of Kells, south of Kilkenny City, is one of the most striking buildings in Ireland. It was founded in 1193 by Geoffrey FitzRobert de Marisco and run by the Augustinian order. Although called a priory this was both a spiritual and a commercial undertaking. Kells generated a great deal of industry and the priory complex incorporated a mill and brewery. Even visually Kells Priory is different: the church, dormitory, library and other structures one would expect at a monastery are surrounded by a massive wall and a number of medieval towers that give the priory the appearance of a fortress.

These fortifications however make sense considering that Kells Priory was sacked and burned on several occasions. In 1252 by Lord William de Birmingham, in 1316 by Lord Edward Bruce and in 1327 by Maurice Fitzgerald, Earl of Desmond. The end for Kells, like for many other monastic settlements, came in 1540 with the Dissolution of Monasteries and forty years later with the arrival of Cromwell.

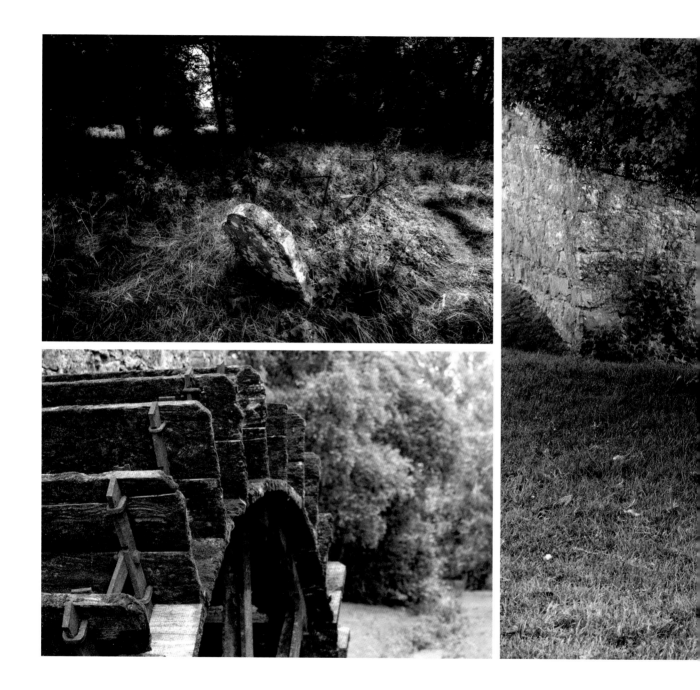

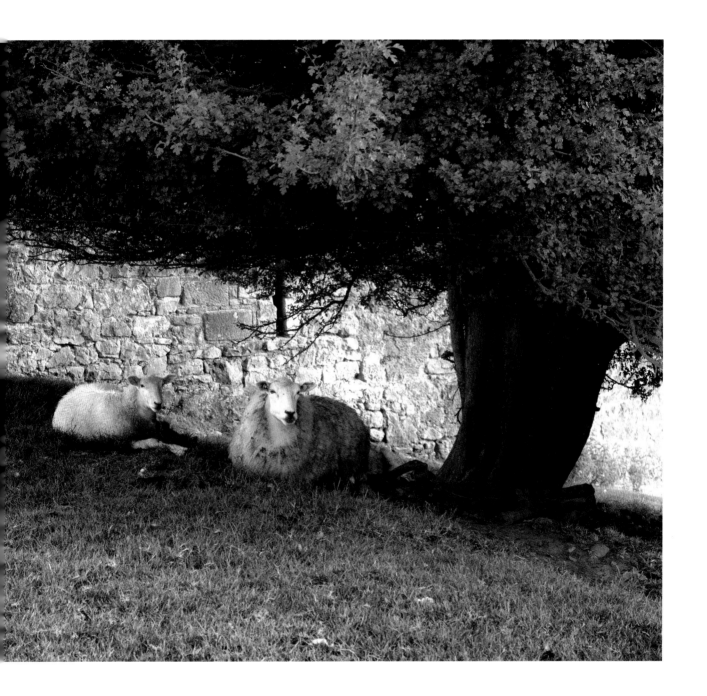

Left page top: Old Graveyard, Kells Priory, Co. Kilkenny
Left page bottom: Mullins Mill, Kells, Co. Kilkenny
Right page: Sheep, Kells Priory, Co. Kilkenny

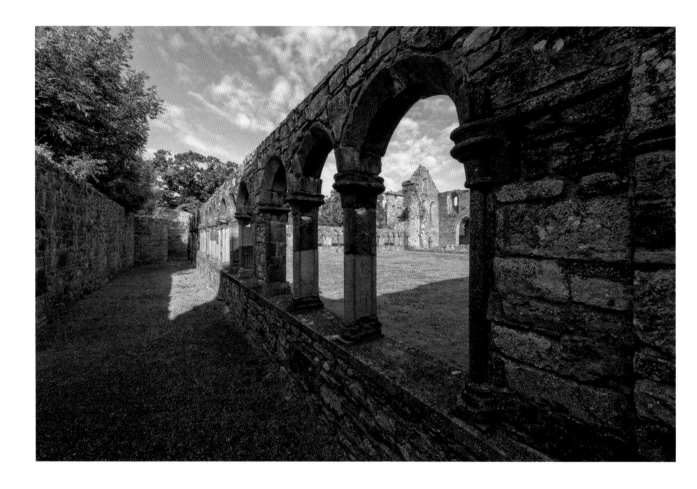

Left page: Cloister, Jerpoint Abbey, Co. Kilkenny
Right page: Jerpoint Abbey, Co. Kilkenny

Jerpoint Abbey was founded in 1160 and taken over by the Cistercian order in 1180. Twenty years later William Pembroke, Earl Marshal of Kilkenny Castle, decided to build a town just across the river from the abbey. His imagination in naming the town unfortunately didn't live up to his ambition in building it: He called it 'Nova Villa Juxta Geripons', which means 'the new town across from Jerpoint' or 'Newtown Jerpoint' for short.

Despite the lengthy and unimaginative name the town flourished up to the 17th century. Today not much is left of the town, but one legend lives on: Santa Claus is allegedly buried in the small parish churchyard of Newtown Jerpoint.

Santa Claus or St Nicholas, Archbishop of Myra in Turkey, died in 342AD and was buried in his hometown. There he rested in peace until the Norman crusaders arrived. According to legend the DeFreynes, knights of Jerpoint, exhumed the remains of St Nicholas of Myra and brought them to Normandy from where they eventually and somehow found their way to Jerpoint. The parish church of Newtown-Jerpoint was built and dedicated to St Nicholas and it is said that his remains rest under a slab depicting a monk in habit and cowl.

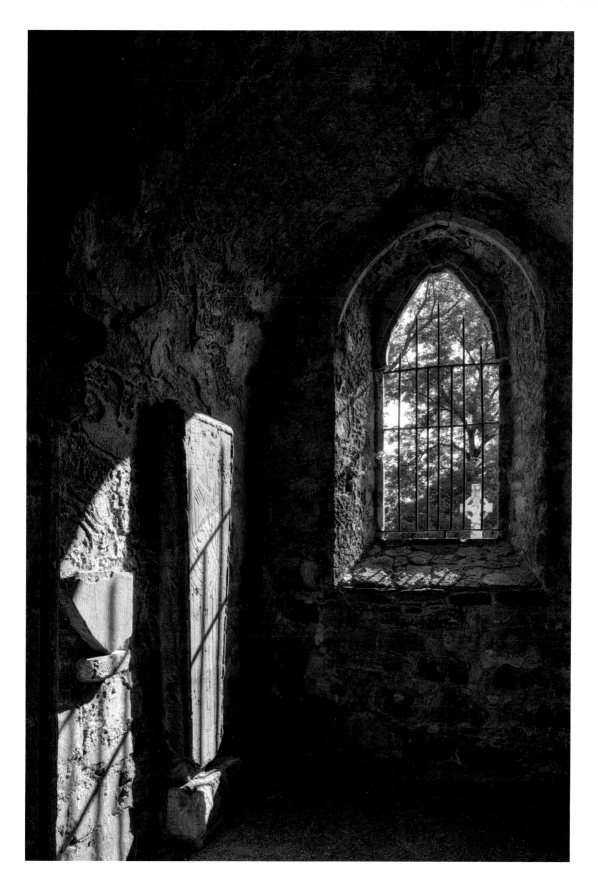

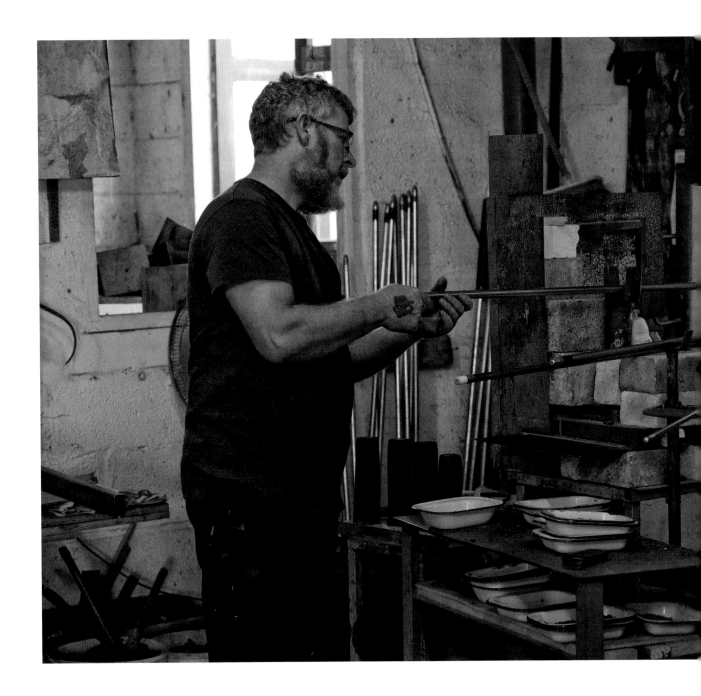

Jerpoint Glass was established in 1979 by Keith and Kathleen Leadbetter and has gained an international reputation. Keith learned his craft in the UK and the prestigious Orrefors Glass School in Sweden and, after travelling extensively through Europe to further develop his skills, settled in Jerpoint. Kathleen is a self-taught artist and responsible for the unique Jerpoint Glass colour palette

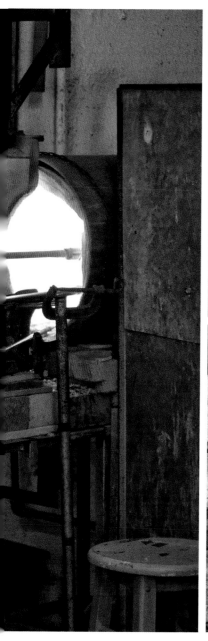

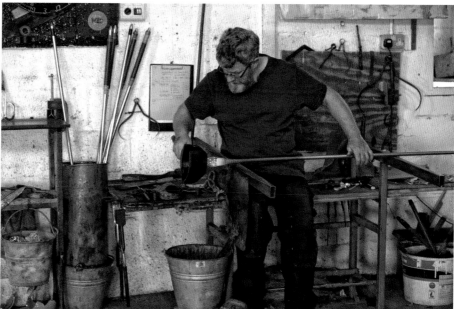

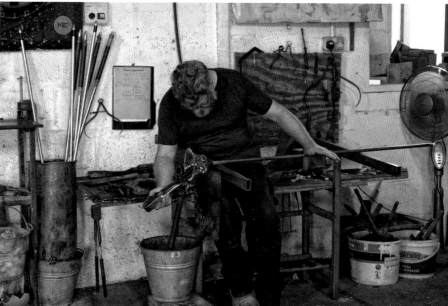

Keith Leadbetter of Jerpoint Glass, Jerpoint, Co. Kilkenny

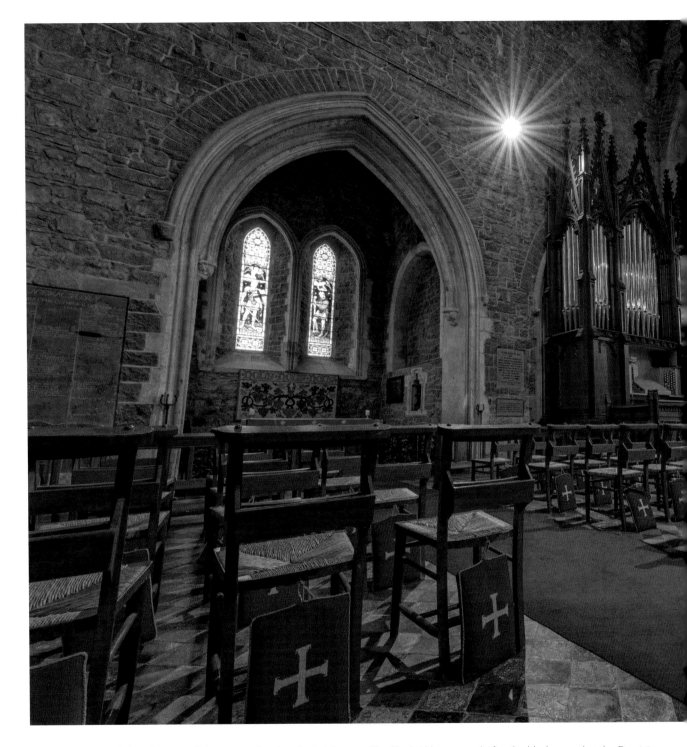

St Canice's Cathedral is the second longest medieval cathedral in Ireland. It occupies the site of the original monastic settlement and was finished in 1285. It is said that Oliver Cromwell destroyed the interior and windows and used the cathedral as a stable for his horses during the occupation of Kilkenny. The flat shelf on top of the round tower is known as 'Cromwell's Seat' and it is easily to imagine Cromwell observing the city from this high viewpoint.

The Black Abbey, named after the black cape that the Dominicans wore over their white habits, suffered a similar fate. The Dominican Abbey was founded in 1225, turned into a courthouse in 1543 during the reformation, only to be seized by the people of Kilkenny sixty years later who returned it to the Dominicans. In 1650 the building was almost entirely destroyed by Cromwell and his forces. It took until 1816 for its doors to open again for the public and until 1979 until restoration was complete. The Black Abbey is still home to the Dominicans today.

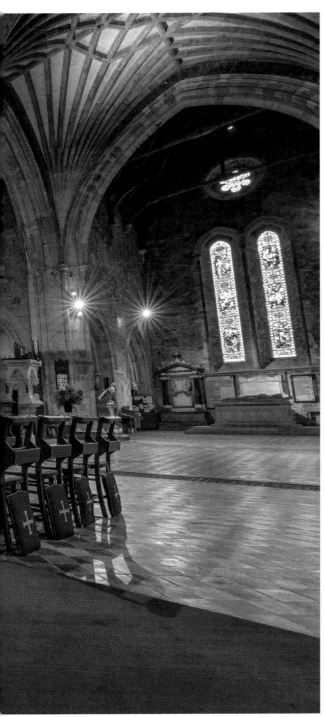

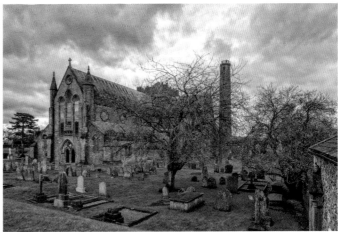

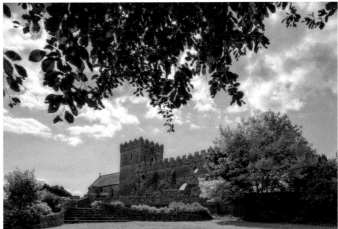

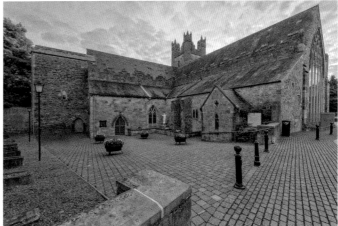

Left page: St Canice's Cathedral, Kilkenny City
Right page top: St Canice's Cathedral, Kilkenny City
Right page centre: St Mary's Church, Gowran, Co. Kilkenny
Right page bottom: Black Abbey, Kilkenny City

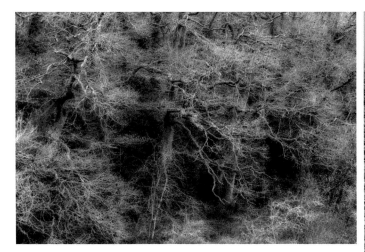

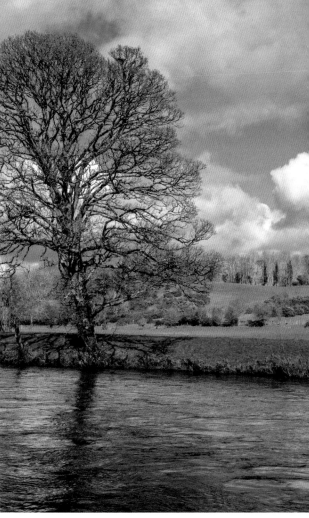

Left page: Winter Woodland, Nore Valley, Co. Kilkenny
Left page right: River Nore near Thomastown, Co. Kilkenny
Right page: Summer Sunset just outside Kilkenny City, Co. Kilkenny

CASTLES AND CONQUESTS

Once upon a time Kilkenny was the most important city in Ireland; some time in the 6th century St Canice or one of his followers established a monastery at an important fording point on the River Nore. The small settlement that sprang up around the church soon grew into a town that became known as *Cill Chainnigh*, the Church of Canice.

After the Anglo Norman invasion of the late 12th century the town was separated into what was known as 'Irishtown', the area around the original foundation, and 'Englishtown' or 'Hightown', the area around the castle.

In 1208 Kilkenny was granted a town charter and in 1266 the Charter of Murage, which allowed for fortified walls, a sign of status and importance. The walls were finished in 1400 and Kilkenny became one of the most important trading centres and military strongholds in Ireland.

In 1366 one of the most notorious pieces of legislation ever written was put into law by the Irish Parliament (which sat in Kilkenny at the time). The goal was to stop the occupying Anglo Normans becoming 'more Irish than the Irish themselves'.

... ore plusors Engleis de la dit terre guepissant la lang gis monture leys & usages Engleis vivent et se governement as maniers guise et lang des Irrois enemies et auxiant ount fait divers mariages & aliaunces enter eux et les Irrois enemyes avauntditz dont le dit terre et le lieg people de icelle la lang Engloies ligeance a nostre seignour le Roy Duc et lez leis Engleis illoeques sont mis en subjection et retrets... (Anglo Norman text).

... now many English of the said land, forsaking the English language, manners, mode of riding, laws and usages, live and govern themselves according to the manners, fashion, and language of the Irish enemies; and also have made divers marriages and alliances between themselves and the Irish enemies aforesaid; whereby the said land, and the liege people thereof, the English language, the allegiance due to our lord the king, and the English laws there, are put in subjection and decayed... (English translation)

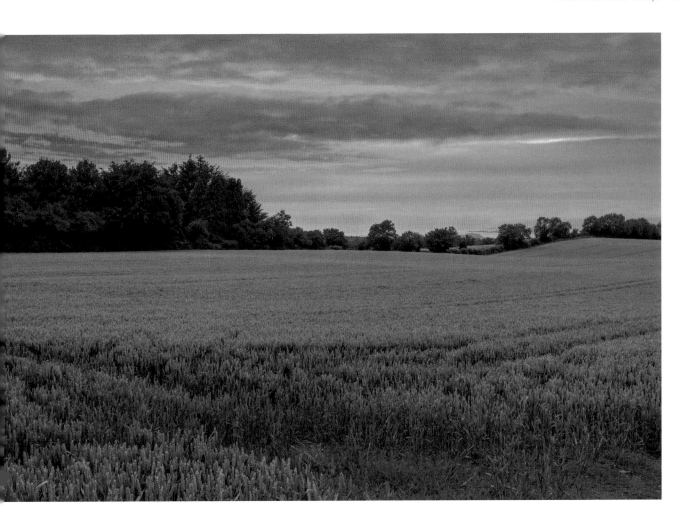

The Statute of Kilkenny, as the legislation became known, forbid, among other things, to cut the hair in Irish style, speak the Irish language, play hurling or other games of Irish origin and form alliancies with the Irish, which included marriage and fostering.

In 1609 King James I granted Kilkenny the status of city. This marked the beginning of a century of extreme prosperity. During this time Kilkenny was ruled by rich merchant families who controlled not only the trade but also every office of church and state in the city.

Archdekin, Archer, Cowley, Langton, Lee; Knaresborough, Lawless, Raggett, Rothe and Shee. These were the families who gave Kilkenny its reputation and built the great houses that survived to this day.

In 1642 Kilkenny became the provisional capital of Ireland. The Catholic uprising in Ulster and civil war in England inspired a gathering of Irish nobility and gentry which led to the formation of a supreme council that would effectively rule Ireland for the following seven years.

In 1649 however the English civil war ended with the execution of King Charles I and one year later Oliver Cromwell arrived in Ireland. After a week-long siege Kilkenny surrendered. The following years witnessed the decline of Kilkenny. The former powerful merchant families were expelled from the city and their properties confiscated.

Some ten years later King Charles II allowed the families to return and try to rebuild Kilkenny's glory days, but things would never be the same. Dublin had taken over the role of political and economic centre and would eventually become the capital city.

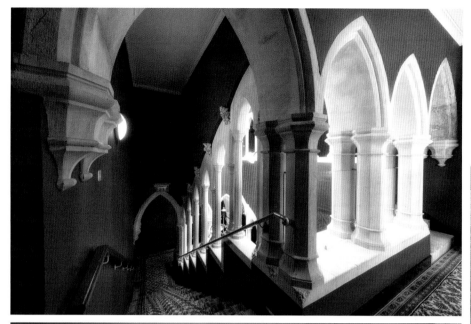

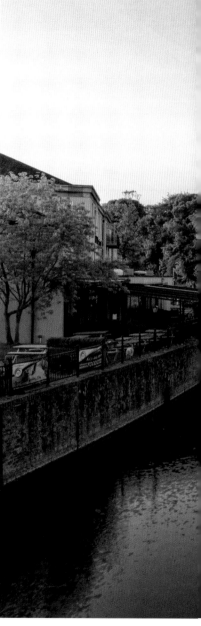

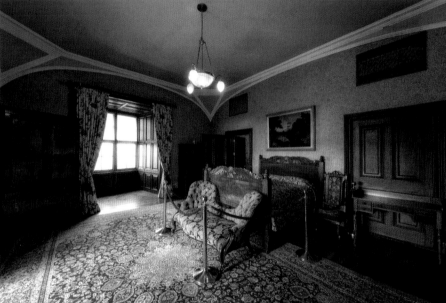

Left page top:: Moorish Staircase, Kilkenny Castle
Left page bottom: Bedroom, Kilkenny Castle
Right page: Kilkenny Castle and River Nore

Shortly after the first Anglo Norman invasion of Ireland Richard de Clare, better known as Strongbow, built a wooden fortification on the present site of Kilkenny Castle. Strongbow's son, William Marshall, built the stone castle between 1192 and 1195. William was also the one who granted the town charter for Kilkenny some years later.

In 1391 James Butler, 3rd Earl of Ormonde, bought Kilkenny Castle from William Marshall's heirs for a mere 800 pounds. The Butler family would occupy the castle for almost 600 years. They left Kilkenny Castle in 1935 and gave it to the people of Kilkenny in 1967 for the nominal sum of 50 pounds.

There are many stories and legends connected with the building, but one of the most enticing is the tale of the Ladies of Llangollen.

Lady Eleanor Butler, born in 1739, was the daughter of the 16th Earl of Ormonde. She was known as a rather independent and rebellious mind and the relationship between her and her family was a bumpy affair.

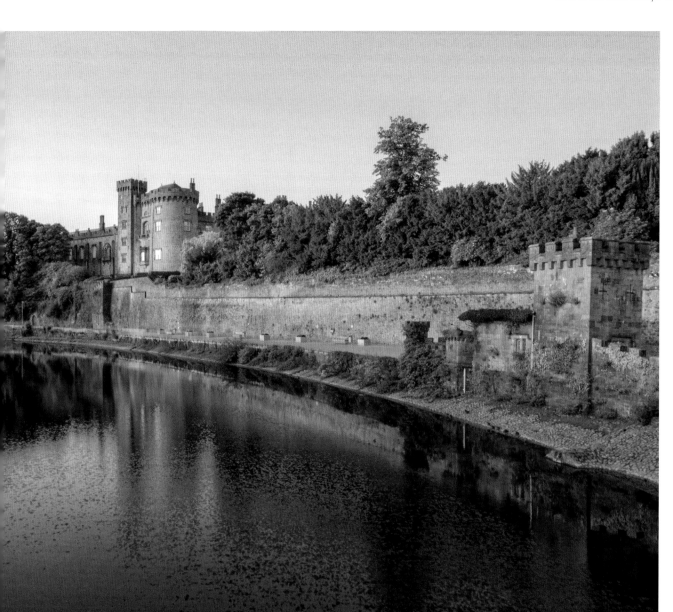

When Eleanor was thirty she met Sarah Ponsonby, a shy, fourteen-year-old schoolgirl. The orphaned Sarah lived with her relations, the Fownes, at Woodstock House in Inistioge, south of Kilkenny City. They became friends and stayed in contact for the years to come.

Sarah had to endure advances of her guardian Sir William Fownes and Eleanor's difficult relationship with her family worsened further. In 1778 Lady Eleanor and Sarah absconded to Waterford. It was a perfect scandal and only two days later the ladies were brought back by their families. Eleanor was sent to stay with relatives under house arrest, but three weeks later she escaped and was found hiding in Sarah's cupboard at Woodstock House.

This time the families sought a final solution for what was considered an unnatural relationship. Lady Eleanor and Sarah were shipped off to Wales with a meagre pension. There in a cottage in Llangollen they spent the rest of their lives together. Eleanor passed away in 1829 and was followed by Sarah only two days later.

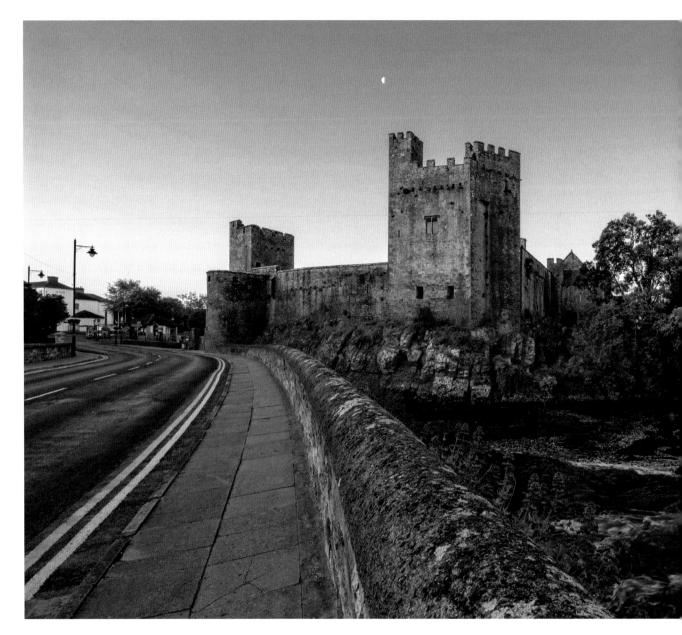

Cahir Castle is one of the largest castles in Ireland, built from 1142 by Conor O'Brien, Prince of Thomond. In 1375 it was granted to James, 3rd Earl of Ormond, a member of the Butler family who left their mark on the Suir Valley for 800 years. Cahir, Clonmel and Carrick on Suir are all connected to the Butler family, the Dukes and Earls of Ormond. The last Butler heir passed away in 1964.

Blackwater Castle near Castletownroche can trace back human habitation to Mesolithic times some 10,000 years ago which makes it one of the oldest permanently-occupied sites in Ireland.

The first settlers lived in caves above the Awbeg River, a tributary of the Blackwater, just opposite from today's castle. Flint stones, *fulachta fiadhs* (outdoor cooking sites) and other artefacts from the Mesolithic and Neolithic have been found in the area. During the Bronze and Iron Age the site featured a promontory fort known as Dun Cruadha. Remains of its defensive walls can are still visible today. The Normans used these structures later as a foundation of their own defensive walls when they settled here around the 12th century. The remaining structures on site today; defensive walls, watch towers, a chapel, the well and the tower house, date from the 12th, 13th and 14th century. Lords of what was then called Roche's Castle were the Roche (or de la Roche) family, Viscounts of Fermoy, who ruled over an extensive tract of land comprising the towns of Mallow, Fermoy and Doneraile over several generations.

The Roche's rule came to a sudden end in during the Cromwellian Invasion. Maurice, Lord Roche, and his wife Lady Ellen Roche, were both devoted Catholics and resisted the new Protestant faith. Maurice was imprisoned in England for his beliefs and after his release and return to Ireland he joined the Irish Rebellion of 1641.

In January 1650 Castle Roche was attacked and eventually taken by Cromwell's troops. The officers who let the defence of the castle were all executed and Lady Roche herself was hanged in 1652 on a trumped-up charge of murder.

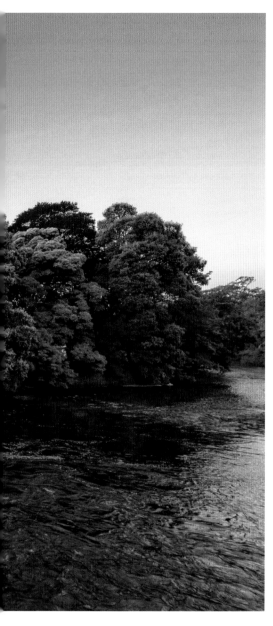

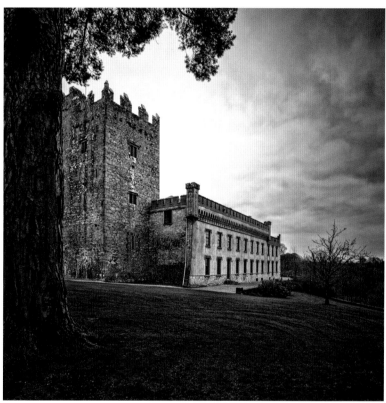

She was brought before one of those High Courts of Justice (or injustice) set up immediately after the surrender of the Irish in 1652 where they hanged women for want of men. There she was tried, condemned and afterwards hanged, on the evidence of a strumpet, for shooting a man with a pistol whose name was unknown to the witness – although it was ready to be proved Lady Roche was twenty miles distant from the spot.

A Brief Narrative of the Sufferings of the Irish under Cromwell – London 1660

Maurice gave himself up in the same year, was dispossessed of his entire estate and died in poverty in 1670.

In 1666 the castle was given to Lieutenant Colonel John Widenham and renamed Castle Widenham. The following 300 years passed peacefully. In 1963 the castle was sold to Lord and Lady Cotter who sold it on in 1976 and from there on the castle went through a number of owners until the Nordstrom family purchased it in 1992 and established the Nordstrom Family Trust.

Left page: Cahir Castle and River Suir, Co. Tipperary
Left page bottom: Blackwater Castle, Castletownroche, Co. Cork

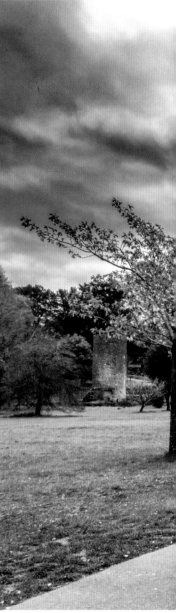

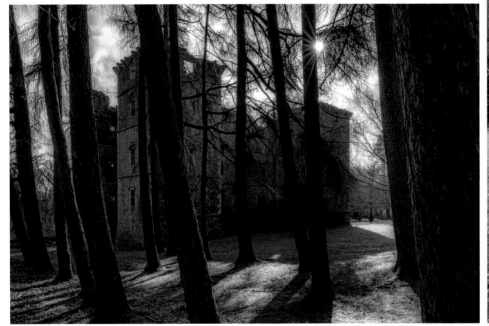

Left page: Kanturk Castle, Co. Cork
Right page: Blarney Castle and Gardens, Co. Cork

Kanturk Castle stands at the outskirts of the market town of the same name close to the confluence of the rivers Allow and Dalua, both tributaries of the Blackwater. It was built around 1600 by MacDonagh McCarthy, but very likely never finished. The story goes that the English stopped the building process out of fear that the castle could be used as a base for an Irish uprising. When MacDonagh was given the news he allegedly smashed all the blue ceramic tiles that were meant for the roof and threw them in a nearby stream. The stream has been known as the Bluepool Stream ever since.

Another legend tells us that all seven stone masons who worked on the castle were named John which locally gave the castle the name *Carrig-na-Shane-Saor*, 'the Rock of John the Mason'.

Blarney Castle is best known for its stone, the Blarney Stone. Kissing the stone endows the kisser with the skill of 'blarney' – flattery and eloquence – it is said. The origins of the stone are shrouded in myth. One story says that Cormac McCarthy, who built the original castle, got involved in a legal battle. He appealed to Cliodhna, goddess and queen of the banshees, for assistance. She told McCarthy to kiss the first stone

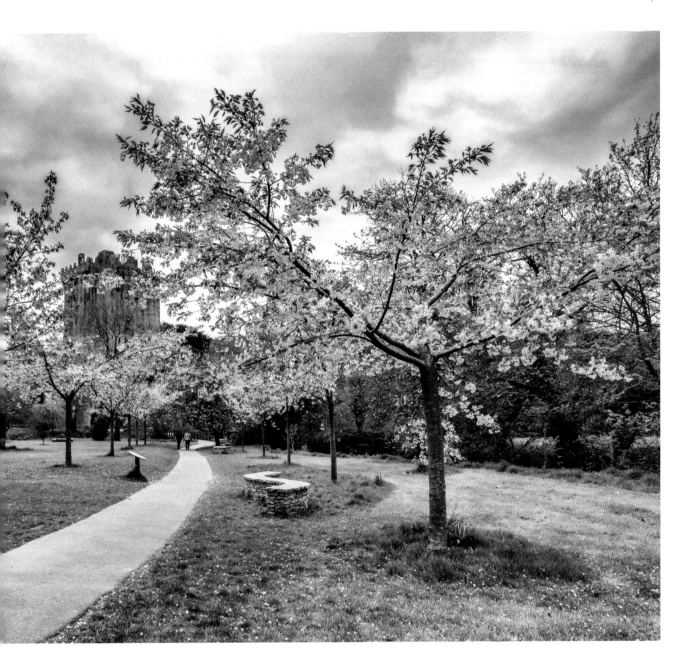

he would find in the morning on his way to court and he did so. As a result he pled his case with great eloquence and won. McCarthy then incorporated the stone into the battlements of his castle. Another story states that the Blarney Stone was once part of the Stone of Scone, also known as the Stone of Destiny or Coronation Stone which was used for centuries in the coronation of the monarchs of Scotland and England. Robert the Bruce allegedly gave part of the stone to McCarthy as a thank you after McCarthy supported Robert at the battle of Bannockburn in 1314.

The name 'Blarney' was said to have been coined by Queen Elizabeth I of England, who wanted the then unnamed castle taken from Cormac McCarthy. The Earl of Leicester who was assigned with the task fell victim to the flattery of McCarthy (who very likely kept kissing the stone on a regular basis) and got nowhere near taken over the castle.

Whenever Queen Elizabeth asked for a progress report all she got was a long missive. This went on for a while and at some stage the irritated queen remarked that the reports were all 'blarney' – pleasant talk, intended to deceive without offending' and the name stuck.

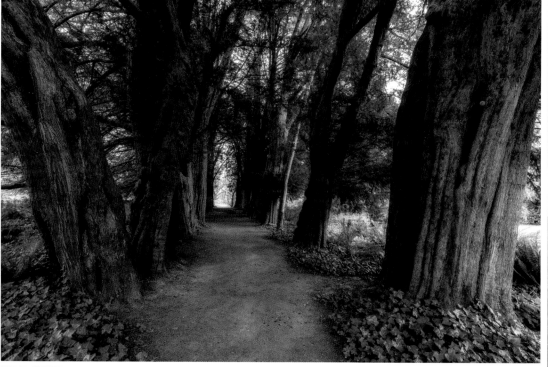

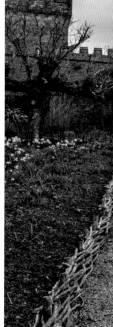

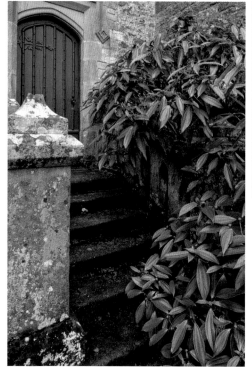

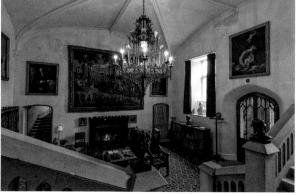

Left page top: Yew Walk, Lismore Castle, Co. Waterford
Left page bottom: Side Door, Lismore Castle, Co. Waterford
Left page right: Drawing Room, Lismore Castle, Co. Waterford
Right page: Lismore Castle and Upper Garden, Co. Waterford

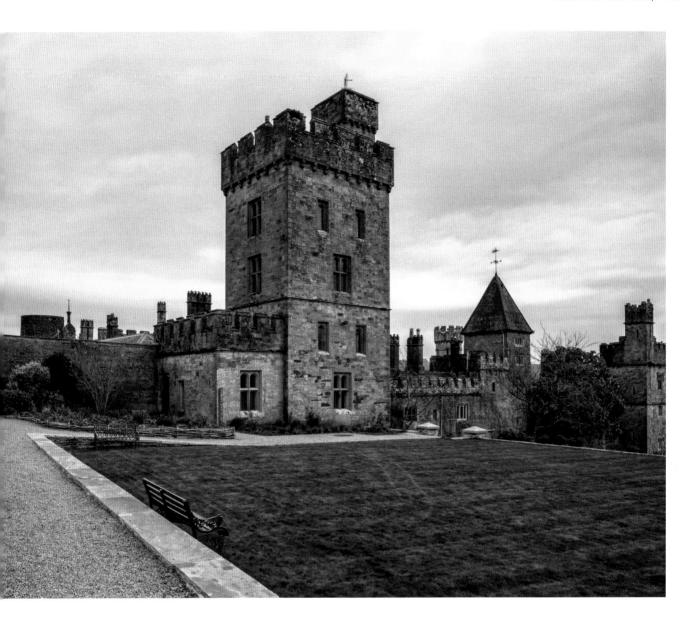

BIG HOUSES AND HARD TIMES

The castle at Lismore would fit perfectly into a fairytale. It was built in 1185 on the site of Lismore Abbey, at the time an important monastery and centre of learning. The first owners, the Earls of Desmond, lost the site after the so-called Desmond Rebellions and the violent death of Gerald FitzGerald, 15th Earl of Desmond in 1583. Sir Walter Raleigh owned Lismore Castle for a short while but sold it to Richard Boyle, who would become 1st Earl of Cork, in 1602. In 1753 the castle went to the Cavendish family, the Dukes of Devonshire who transformed Lismore over several generations into the gothic beauty the castle is today. Today, the gardens are open to the public and can be visited.

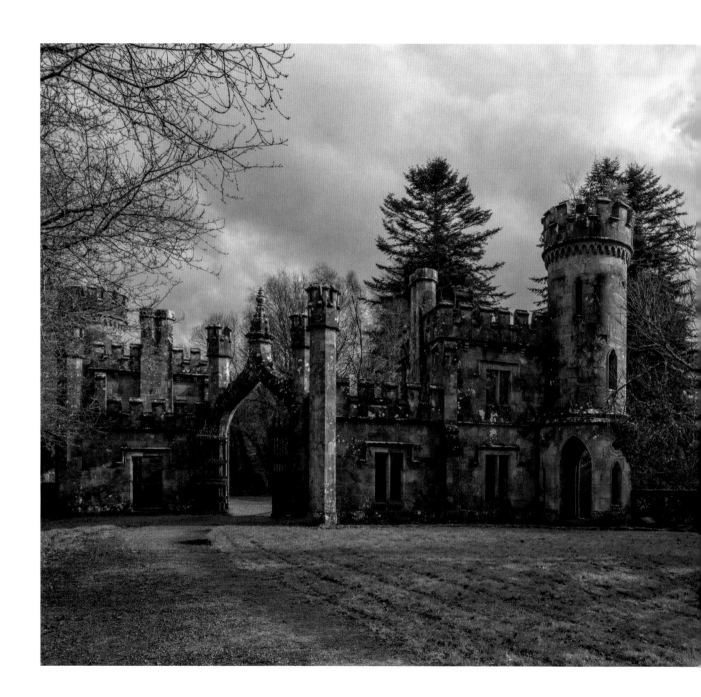

The Ballysaggartmore Towers, located in a woodland just outside Lismore, are an architectural obscurity. They were constructed in the early 19th century for Arthur Kiely-Ussher, a reputedly hard and greedy landlord. Arthur's wife, it is said, wasn't any better and she nagged Arthur into building an extravagant estate that would outshine Strancally Castle, the residence of Arthur's brother John Kiely.

These dreams of grandeur however were soon shattered. After the gate lodge and the tower flanked bridge were finished the Kiely-Usshers run out of money and the great mansion where they would live remained a paper dream. They lived out their days in a modest house and after their deaths the estate was sold on by a liquidator.

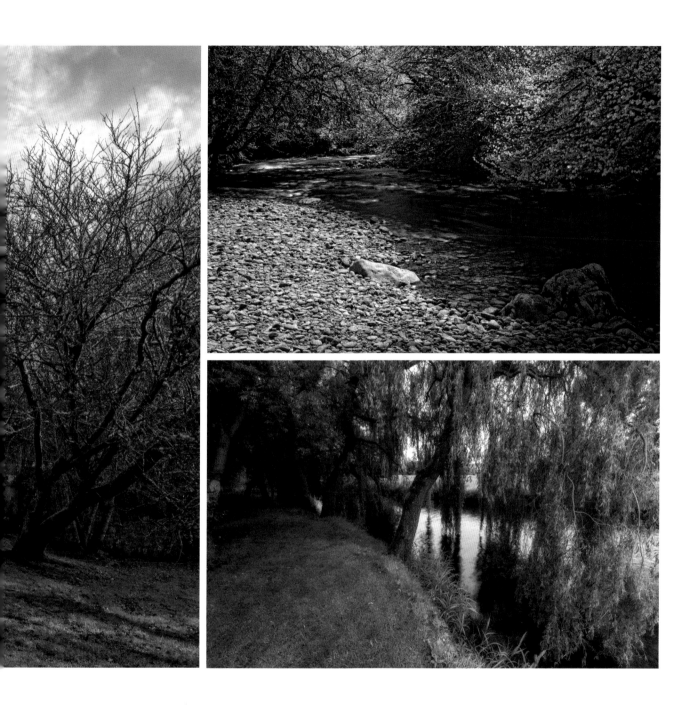

... the crowning folly of them all, at Ballysaggartmore in
Waterford, huge gates, then an even larger bridge, then
for economy a smaller bridge and then at last, no house
for there was no more money, the derelict demesne lies
heavily overgrown, enclosed and silent ...

Contemporary account

Left page: The Towers / Main Gate, Ballysaggartmore, Co. Waterford
Right page top: Owennashed River, Co. Waterford
Right page bottom: Kings River, Co. Kilkenny

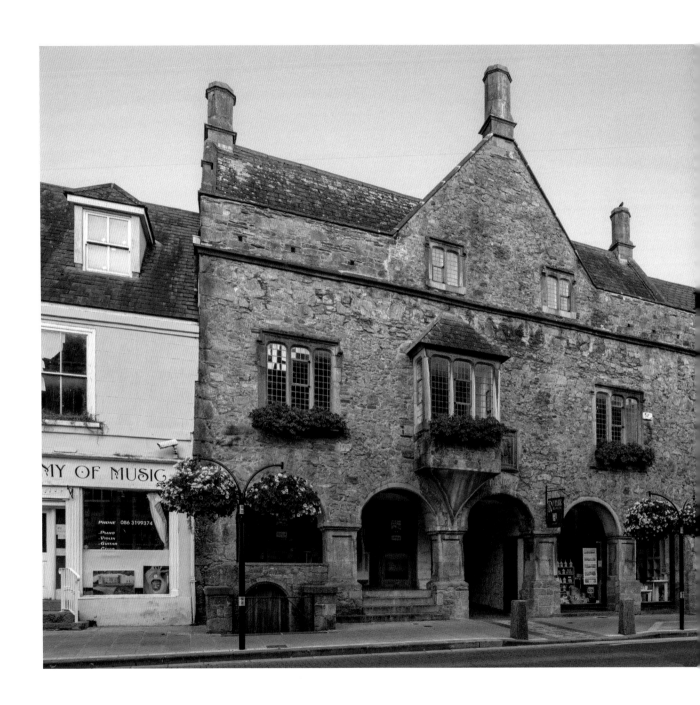

Rothe House is one of the surviving Merchant's Houses of Kilkenny City. It was built in 1594 by John Roth Fitz-Piers and his wife Rose Archer, both members of leading Kilkenny families. The entire complex consists of three houses separated by two courtyards and a garden at the rear of the third house. The Rothe family lost everything under Cromwell's occupation and was sent to Connaught. Later they left Ireland for good.

In the 19th century Rothe House was used as a school and was bought by the Kilkenny Archaeological Society in 1962. After lengthy restoration work Rothe House and its gardens opened to the public.

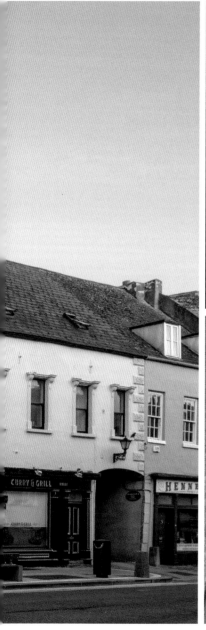

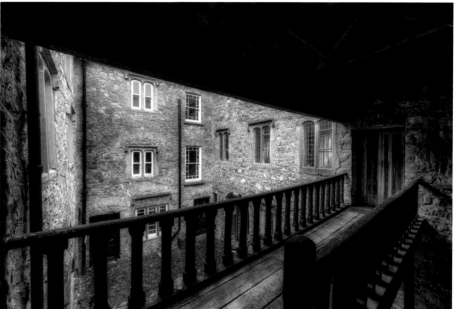

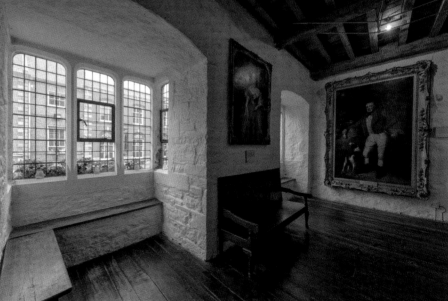

Left page: Rothe House, Kilkenny City
Right page top: Courtyard, Rothe House, Kilkenny City
Right page bottom: The Phelan Room, Rothe House, Kilkenny City

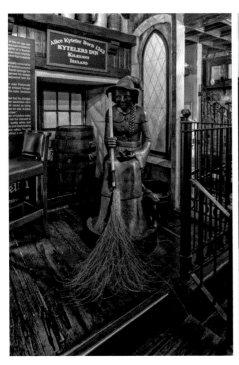
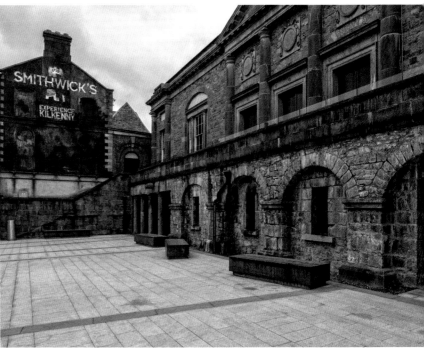

Left page: Alice Kyteler's Statue, Kyteler's Inn, Kilkenny City
Left page centre: Courthouse and Smithwicks Brewery, Kilkenny City
Right page: Kyteler's Inn, Kilkenny City

The legend of Dame Alice Kyteler, Kilkenny's witch, is the stuff of Hollywood movies. Alice was born in 1280 to wealthy parents and lived at Kyteler's Hall, now Kyteler's Inn, and didn't resemble what you would expect from a medieval witch; she wasn't a toothless, wart-ridden old hag, on the contrary she was described as attractive, resourceful and intelligent.

Alice Kyteler had four husbands, three of whom died under very mysterious circumstances leaving her extremely wealthy, well-connected and influential in the community. Her stepchildren on the other hand were left with nothing. In 1324 the state of her fourth husband was described as follows: '... *totally emaciated, deprived of his nails and his hair fell out...*' All are classic symptoms of arsenic poisoning.

In the same year Alice's stepchildren filed a complaint with the Bishop of Ossory, Richard de Ledrede. They accused Alice of witchcraft and murder.

The bishop seized the opportunity to stage a witchcraft trial. He attempted to arrest Dame Alice, her natural son William Outlawe and several of her friends. What Richard de Ledrede didn't expect however was how influential Alice was in Kilkenny. She managed to turn the

tables and got the Bishop arrested and imprisoned in Kilkenny Castle for seventeen days. After his release Bishop Ledrede pressed ahead with his charges and eventually his campaign gained fruit, an arrest warrant for Alice was granted and a date for a full-blown witchcraft trial was set.

The list of accusations was long including the first claim of a witch lying with her incubus: '*Ricardus Ledered, episcopus Ossoriensis, citavit Aliciam Ketil, ut se purgaret de heretica pravitate; quae magiae convicta est, nam certo comprobatum est, quendam demonem incubum (nomine Robin Artisson) concubuisse cum ea ...*' - '*...that is, that Kyteler had intercourse with a demon named as "Robin Artisson"...*'.

The trial, however, never took place. Dame Alice disappeared and was never heard of again. It is thought that she spent the rest of her days somewhere in England.

Alice's son William however was convicted and ordered to attend three masses every day and give alms to the poor. In stark contrast to this light sentence Alice's less well-off maid Petronella was tortured, whipped and eventually burned at the stake.

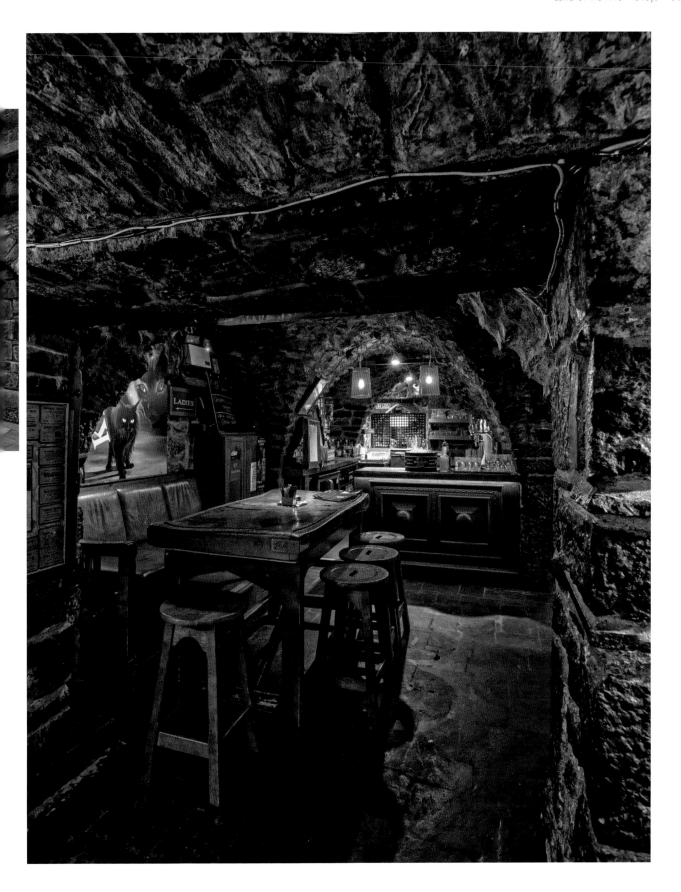

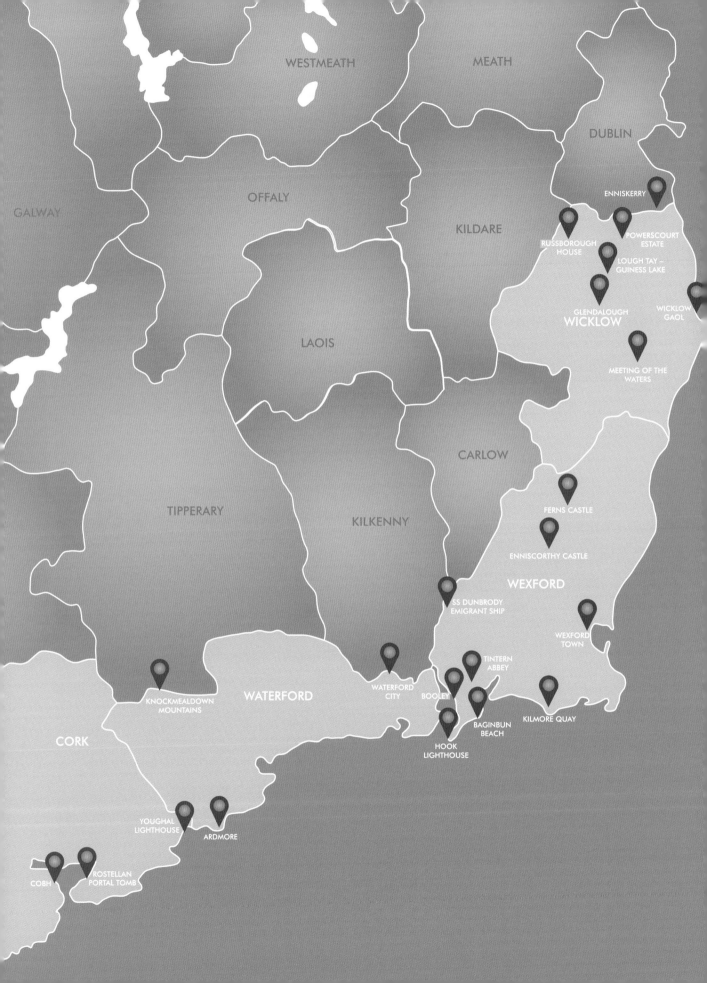

WESTMEATH

MEATH

DUBLIN

GALWAY

OFFALY

KILDARE

ENNISKERRY

RUSSBOROUGH
HOUSE

POWERSCOURT
ESTATE

LOUGH TAY –
GUINESS LAKE

GLENDALOUGH
WICKLOW

WICKLOW
GAOL

MEETING OF THE
WATERS

LAOIS

LAOIS

CARLOW

TIPPERARY

KILKENNY

FERNS CASTLE

ENNISCORTHY CASTLE

WEXFORD

SS DUNBRODY
EMIGRANT SHIP

WEXFORD
TOWN

WATERFORD CITY

WATERFORD

TINTERN
ABBEY

BOOLEY

KILMORE QUAY

KNOCKMEALDOWN
MOUNTAINS

BAGINBUN
BEACH

CORK

HOOK
LIGHTHOUSE

YOUGHAL
LIGHTHOUSE

ARDMORE

COBH

ROSTELLAN
PORTAL TOMB

VIKING COUNTRY

ANCIENT IRELAND

Located at the edge of Cork Harbour, Rostellan portal tomb is Ireland's only 'tidal tomb' and more or less disappears under water with every high tide. It's not the easiest place to reach – getting there involves a hike through Rostellan Wood, through thick undergrowth and along the shore over soft mud – but it's very much worth it.

Bullaun Stones, also known as 'cursing stones' or 'curing stones', date from the Neolithic era, but are often found at Christian sites and have become associated with specific saints. These stones feature one or more hollows ('bullauns'), hence their name, which roughly translates as 'bowl stone'. The water that accumulates in these hollows is said to have healing properties; on the other hand, turning or rolling a Bullaun Stone could curse someone.

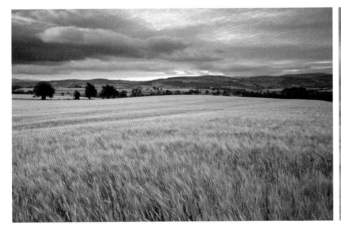
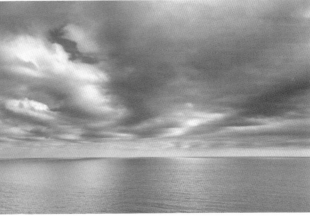

Above left: Knockmealdown Mountains, Co. Waterford
Above right: Sea and Sky, Co. Waterford

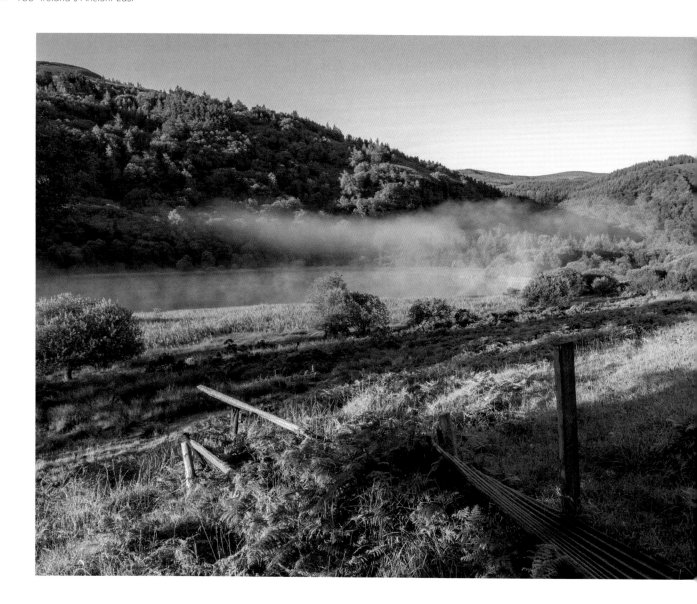

SACRED IRELAND

But in the evening the hills turn blue. White mists rise in the hollows and lie there like thin veils hung from hill to hill. The sun sets. And there is no sound but the wind blowing through the tough grass and the thin trickle of water running through the valleys.

H.V. Morton, *In search of Ireland*

The valley of Glendalough is a place that will stay in your mind forever. From the gates of the valley, which are still guarded by the old monastic city, the tree-covered hills at either side rise steadily while you follow the Poulanass River. Once you have passed the lower lake the valley narrows and the river eventually enters the upper lake. If you visit on a clear dawn you will witness the first sunlight finding its way across the bare mountainside at the head of the valley while veils of fog dance across the surface of the lake.

The valley of Glendalough was formed during the last ice age when glaciers carved deep into the landscape. When temperatures eventually rose the melting ice revealed Glendalough and other valleys like Cloghoge and Glendasan in the vicinity. Glendalough – in Irish, Gleann dá Loch, which translates as 'The Valley of the two Lakes' was formed when sediment divided the original meltwater lake in two.

The story of Glendalough's Monastic City begins in the year 545AD at the Upper Lake. The man who became later known as St Kevin, a descendant of the ruling Leinster families, was following a calling to devote his life to God. According to legend, however, a young woman named Kathleen had fallen madly in love with the future saint and pursued him to the shores of the Upper Lake. The cruel version of the legend tells us that Kevin pushed poor Kathleen into the lake to get rid of her, the less harsh version states that he waited for Kathleen to fall asleep and then rubbed her with stinging nettles. Either way the poor maiden was out of the picture.

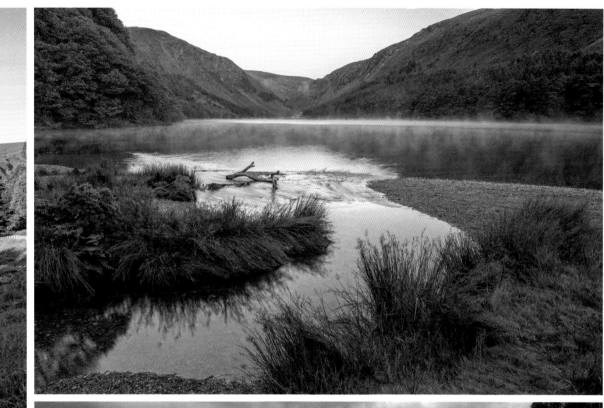

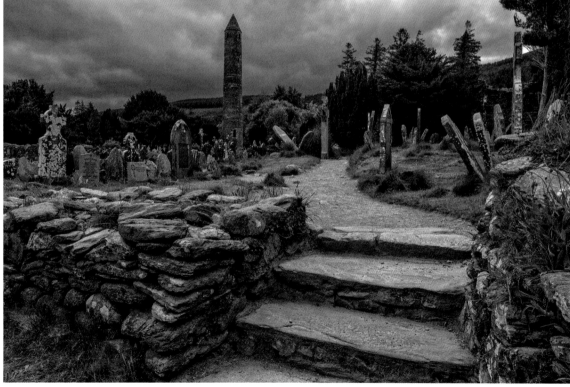

Left page: Lower Lake, Glendalough, Co. Wicklow
Right page top: Upper Lake, Glendalough, Co. Wicklow
Right page bottom: Monastic City, Glendalough, Co. Wicklow

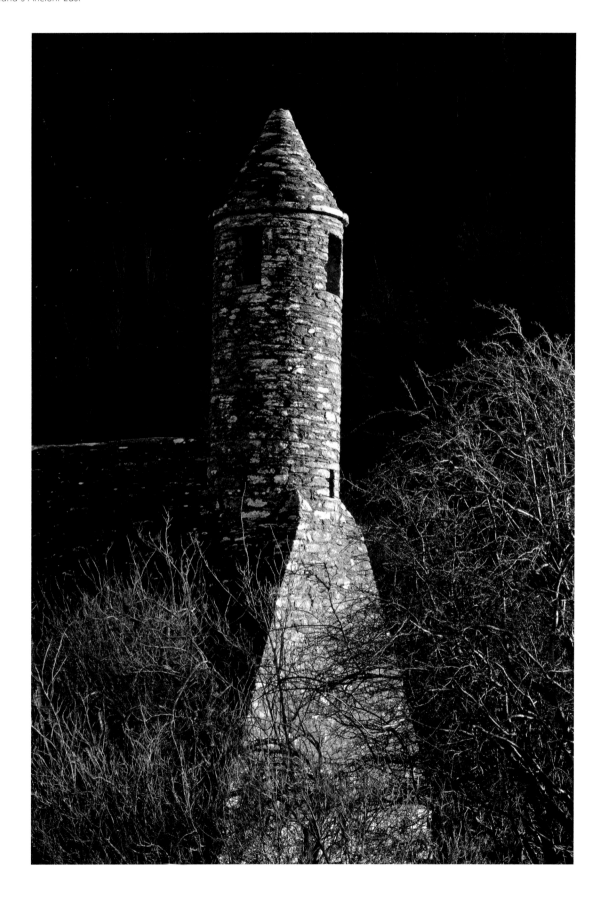

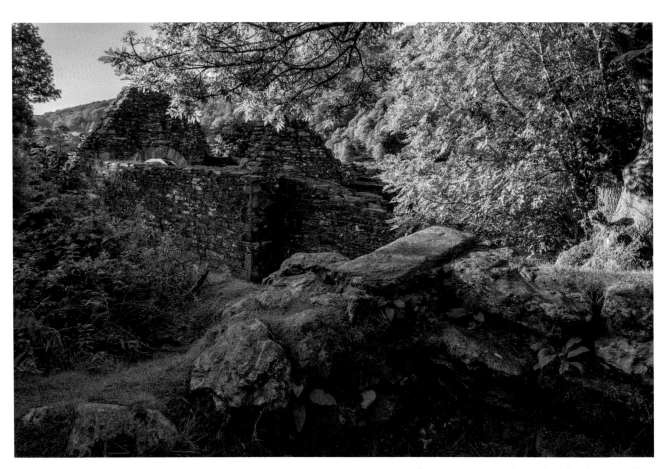

Left page: St Kevin's Kitchen, Glendalough, Co. Wicklow
Right page: Trinity Church, Glendalough, Co. Wicklow

As was not uncommon at the time, St Kevin spent the first years at Glendalough as a hermit in a small cave in the rock face about 8 metres above the lake before he moved into a small beehive hut nearby. The cave, known as St Kevin's Bed, can still be seen today, but can only be reached by boat; t'is said that it was used again as a retreat in the 10th century by St. Laurence O'Toole, abbot of Glendalough and later archbishop of Dublin. St. Kevin, with his extraordinary rapport with wild creatures, is the Irish Francis of Assisi. Allegedly an otter supplied him with fresh salmon every day and another story goes that a blackbird built its nest on St Kevin's outstretched hand. Kevin, as a penance, waited motionless until the eggs had hatched. Eventually St Kevin moved into the lower valley where he founded what would become the Glendalough Monastic City, one of the most influential and long-lived monasteries in Ireland. In its heyday the monastery consisted of seven churches, a round tower, workshops, guest houses, an infirmary, farm buildings and dwellings for both monks and a large lay population. A circular wall surrounded the settlement. Today only the gateway and parts of the wall survive together with some buildings that date from the 10th to 12th century.

The most eye-catching building is probably St. Kevin's Church which is also known as St Kevin's Kitchen: a barrel-vaulted oratory with a steeply pitched room and a round tower belfry. Close to St Kevin's kitchen stands the round tower that rises 30 metres above ground and originally had 6 floors connected by ladders. Round towers were mainly built as bell towers and refuge in times of attack and Glendalough had its fair share of Viking attacks during the centuries.

Other buildings on the grounds include the Cathedral of St Peter & St Paul, the largest of the churches; the Priest's House which was reconstructed from original stones based on a 1779 sketch; St Kieran's Church, named after the founder of Clonmacnoise; St Mary's or Our Lady's Church, one of the earliest and best constructed of the churches, the Trinity Church and St Saviour's Church, the most recent of the Glendalough churches built in the 12th century.

Despite its remote character Glendalough is easily accessible with signposted walks and two parking areas, one near the monastic city and one near the upper lake.

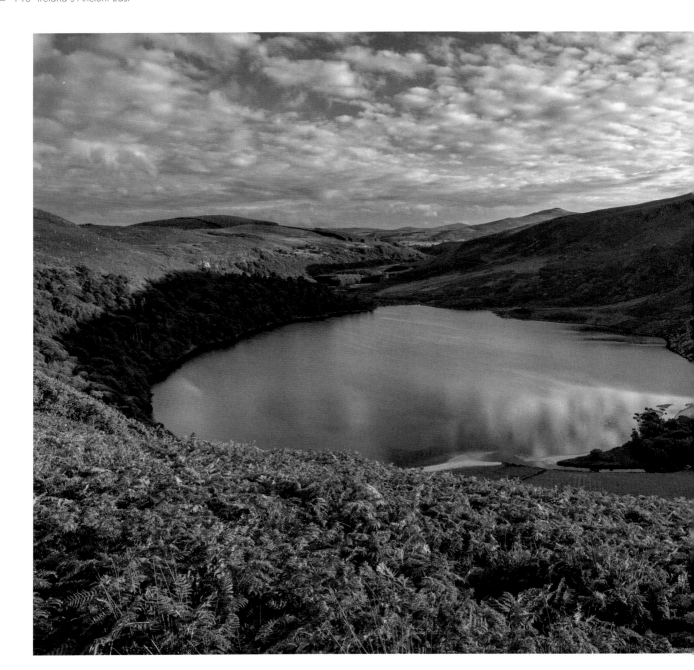

Left page: Lough Tay, Wicklow Mountains, Co. Wicklow
Right page top: Cloghlea Woods, Co. Wicklow
Right page bottom: Winter in the Wicklow Mountains, Co. Wicklow

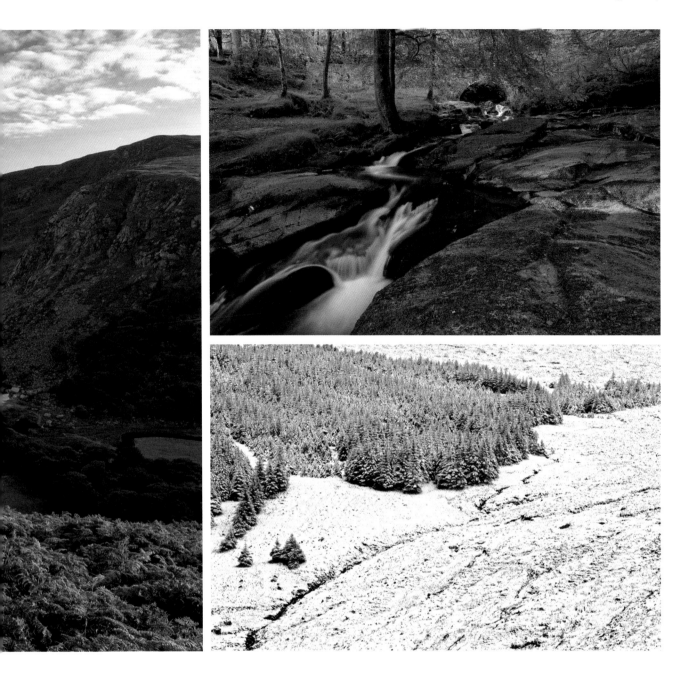

The Wicklow Mountains National Park is one of six National Parks in Ireland, but the only one in the eastern half of the country. It was established in 1991 and today covers more than 200 square kilometres that can be explored by car or on foot on the Wicklow Way. Stretches of blanket bog, native woodland made of oak, ash, rowan and hazel, lakes and rivers and exposed rocky mountain tops are all part of the park.

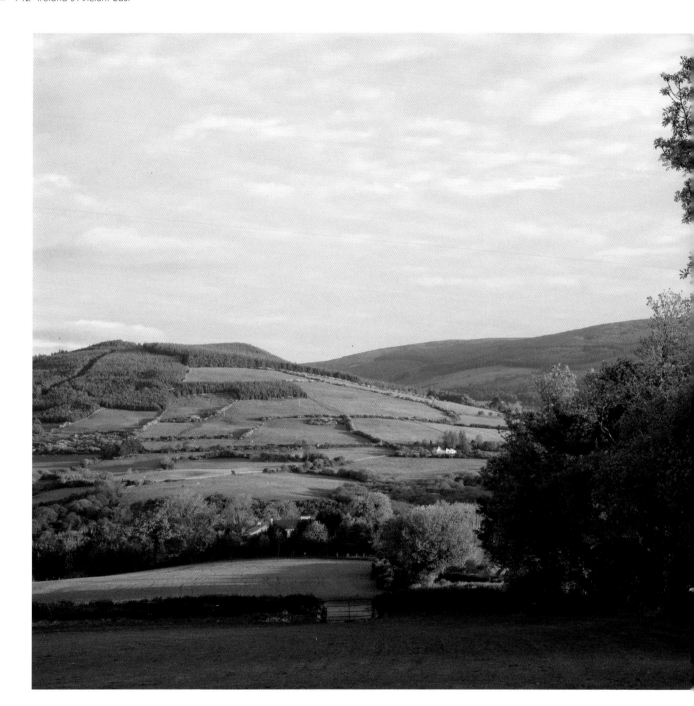

Left page: Countryside, Co. Wicklow
Right page top: Wicklow Mountains Sunset, Co. Wicklow
Right page centre: Glenmacnass Waterfall, Co. Wicklow
Right page bottom: Country Road and Great Sugarloaf, Co. Wicklow

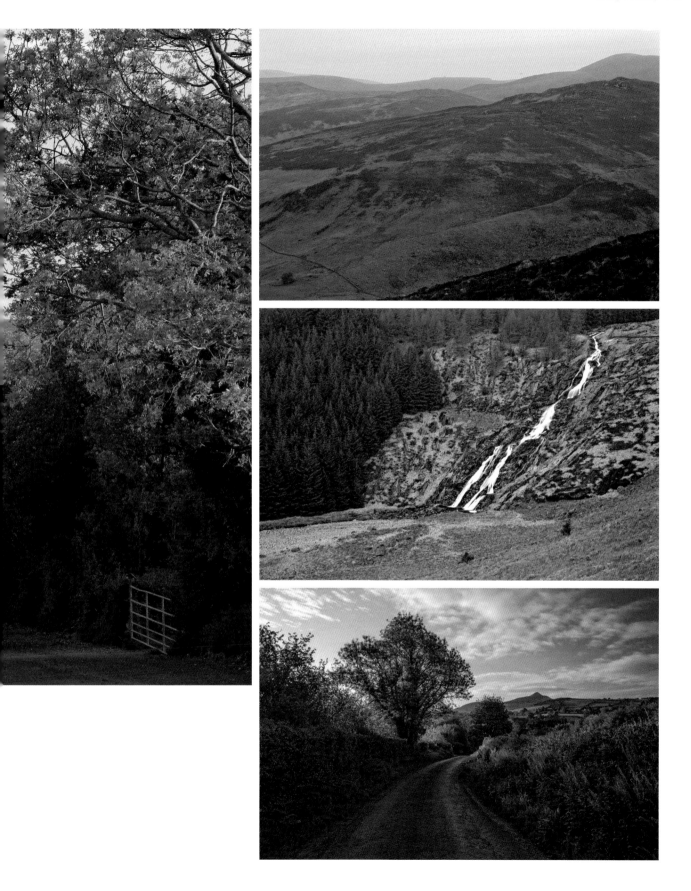

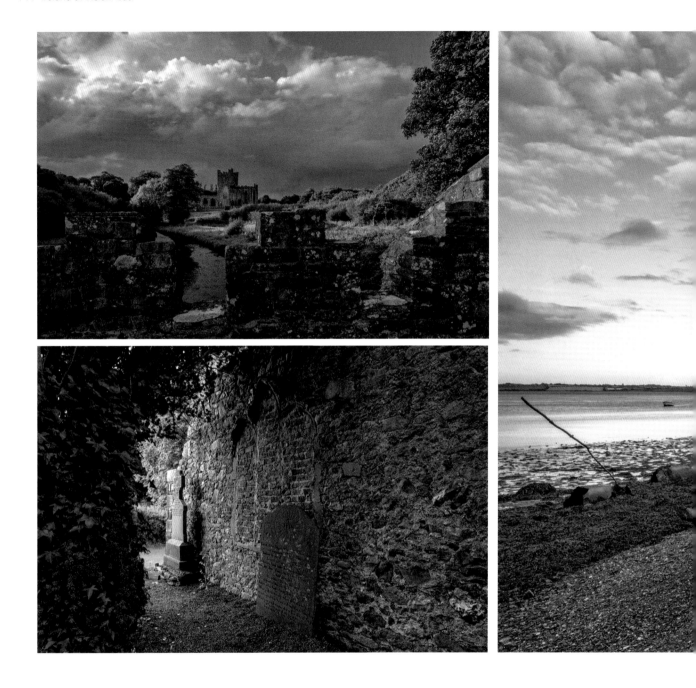

Tintern Abbey was founded in 1200 by William Marshall, who is also responsible for Hook Lighthouse. On his first journey to Ireland as the Lord of Leinster his ship was caught in very bad weather and got close to foundering. William vowed to found a monastery wherever he landed, should he safely reach the shore. Somehow the ship made it to Bannow Bay and William honoured his vow by giving a vast stretch of land to the Cistercian Order. William was also the patron of Tintern Abbey in Monmouthshire in Wales and therefor called this new Cistercian settlement *Tintern de Voto*, 'Tintern of the Vow'.

Tintern of the Vow soon became one of the richest monasteries in the country. After the Dissolution of the Monasteries Tintern was given to Anthony Colclough of Staffordshire. The takeover of the abbey by the Colclough family, however, has been marked by a sinister event. When Anthony Colclough took up residence at the abbey he found that a number of monks still occupied Tintern and he ordered them to be put to death. One of the monks with his last breath put a curse of 'fire and water' on the Colclough family. This curse meant that no member of the Colclough family should ever lead a happy life; instead they would find a violent

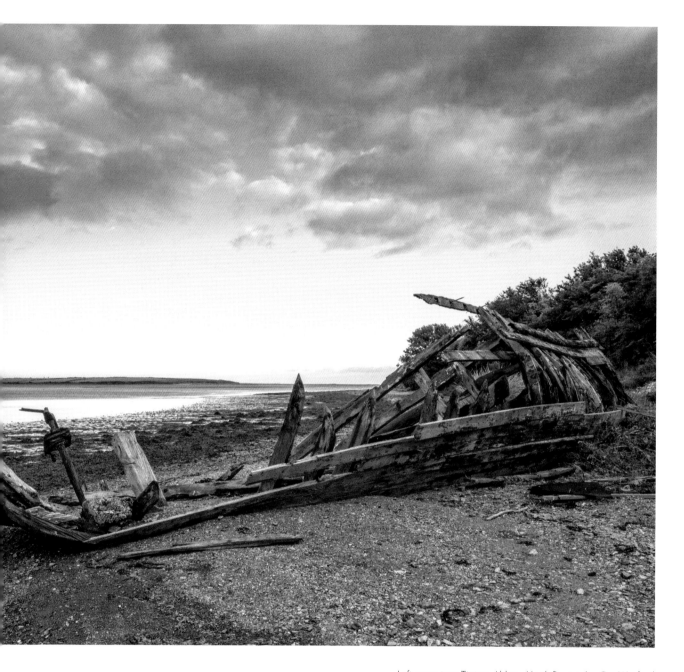

Left page top: Tintern Abbey, Hook Peninsula, Co. Wexford
Left page bottom: Old Graveyard, Tintern, Hook Peninsula, Co. Wexford
Right page: Bannow Bay, Hook Peninsula, Co. Wexford

death. Looking at the family history the curse seemed to have had some effect: four Colcloughs were killed in duels, two were hanged, three died in battle, two were killed in riding accidents and one was killed by his wife. Despite their fate the Colclough family converted Tintern into a domestic home and added walls and towers around the original building. The last member of the Colclough family, Lucey Marie Biddulph Colclough, left Tintern in 1959.

Over the decades it has been reported that the abbey is haunted by the apparition of monks and chanting echoing through the old walls.

During archaeological excavations in the 1980s more than fifty skeletons were found in shallow graves directly under the Colclough residence. It could well be that these are the victims of Anthony Colclough who can't find peace ...

Today the abbey and a number of surviving outbuildings, including a flour mill, castellated bridge and church, are open to the public.

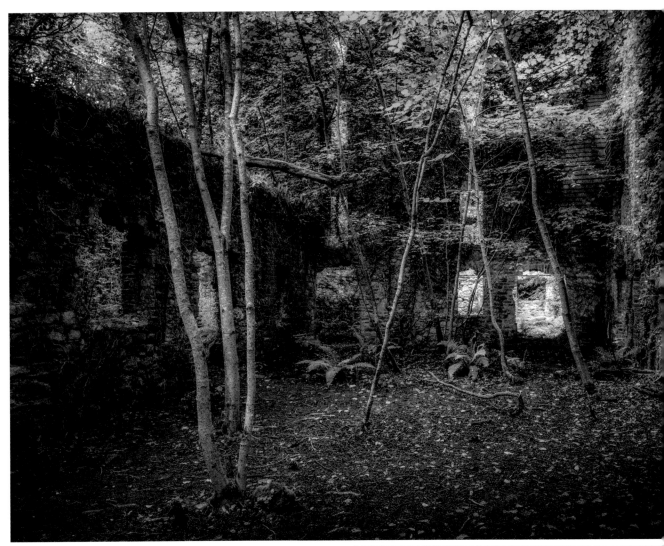

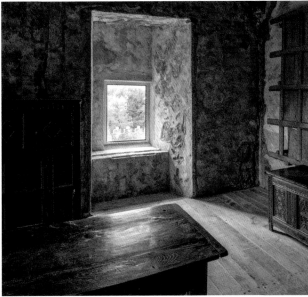

Left page top: The Mill, Tintern, Hook Peninsula, Co. Wexford
Left page bottom: Tintern Abbey Interior, Hook Peninsula, Co. Wexford
Right page: Trees, Tintern, Hook Peninsula, Co. Wexford

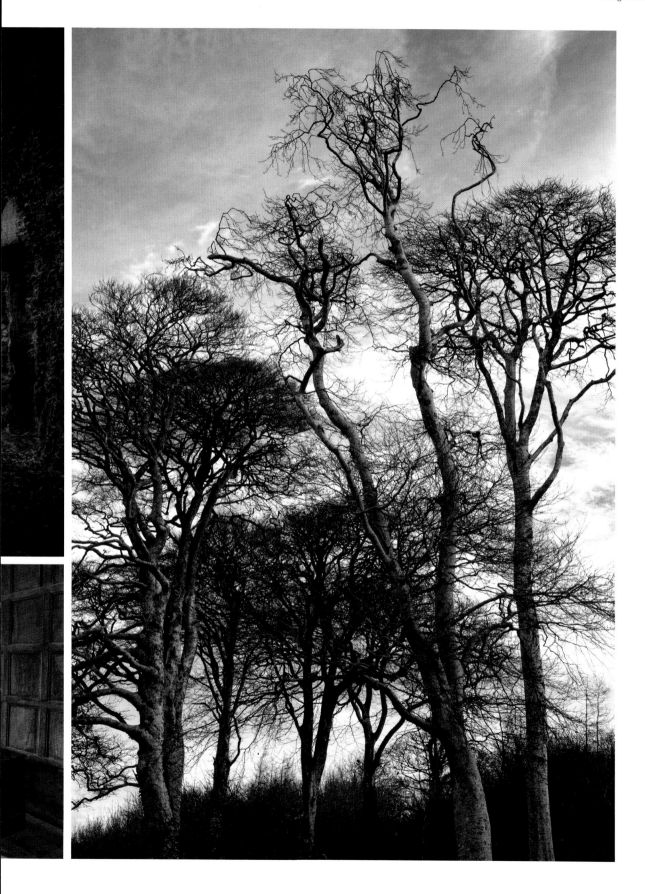

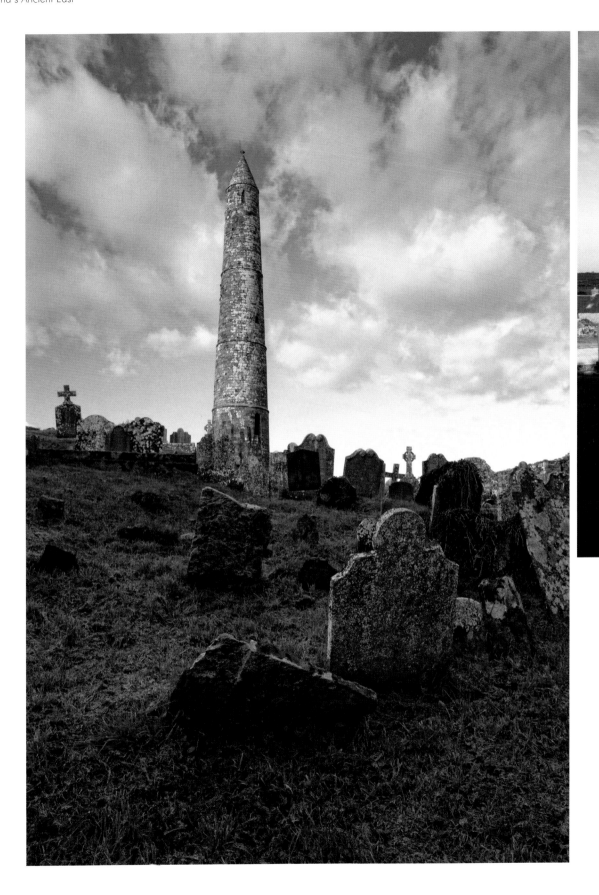

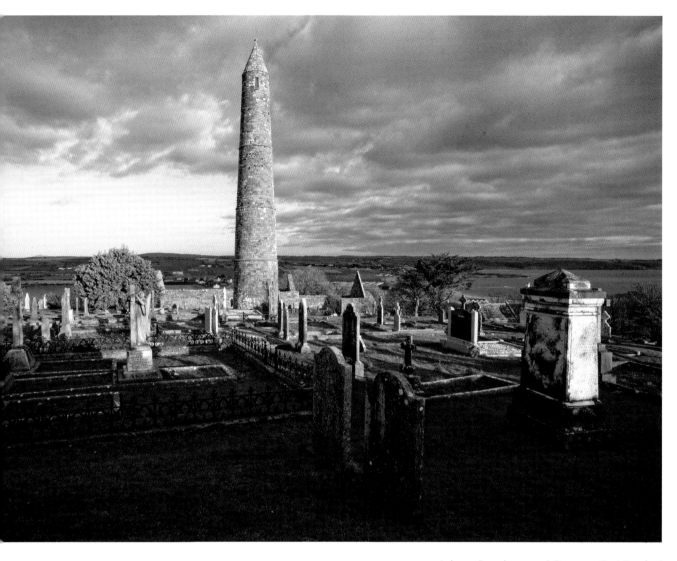

Ardmore Roundtower and Cemetery, Co. Waterford

The monastic settlement at Ardmore dates from around the 5th century and its story goes like this: St Declan was on his way home from his studies in Rome. After he had boarded the boat that would bring him from Wales to Ireland he realised that he had forgotten his bell. The bell it is said was a gift from Heaven and therefore very precious to Declan. Declan's prayers for the safe return of the bell didn't remain unanswered. Halfway across the journey the people on board discovered a boulder with the bell on top sailing in front of their boat. Declan recognised this sign and told his crew to follow the boulder and bell and vowed to establish his monastery wherever the bell led him.

They eventually made landfall in the west of Co. Waterford and after ascending a hill one of Declan's companions wondered doubtfully if it was wise to set up the monastery on this little height. Declan is said to have replied: 'don't call it a little hill, call it a great height: *Ard Mór*'.

The buildings on the site today date from the 8th century (St Declan's Oratory) and 12th century (the Cathedral and Round Tower).

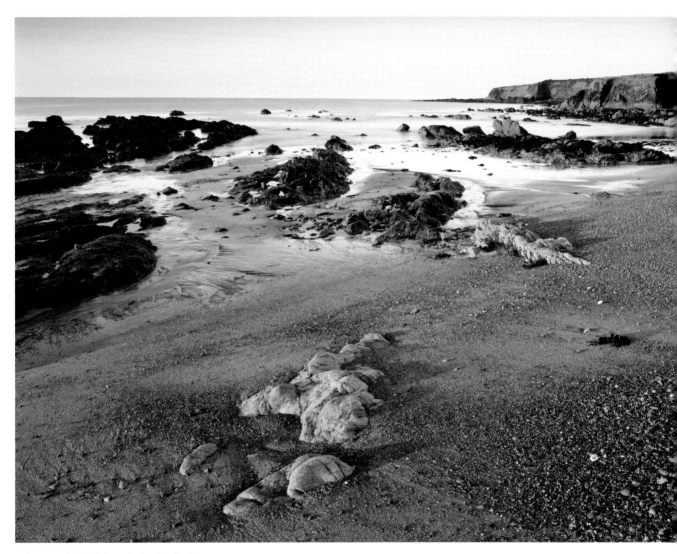

Left page: Blackhall Strand, Co. Wexford
Right page: Ballyvooney Cove, Copper Coast, Co. Waterford

VIKINGS

In 794 AD bands of warriors from Scandinavia arrived in Ireland in search of gold and treasure. Their first target was Rathlin Island off the northern coast, but the Vikings soon extended their area of operations to all Irish coastal waters. Their victims were mostly the rich monasteries and their raids were quick, effective and violent. Everything of value, including food, was taken away and those they did not kill were sold into slavery. These raids went on for some decades, but were only the beginning.

Fierce and wild is the wind tonight,
It tosses the tresses of the sea to white,
On such a night I take my ease,
Fierce Northmen only course the quiet seas.
Scribbled on the margin of a manuscript by an unknown monk

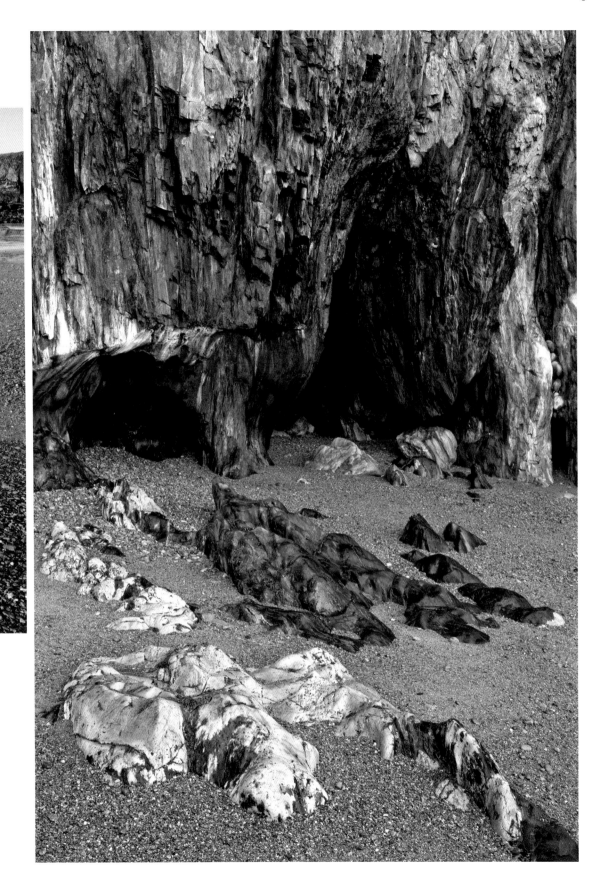

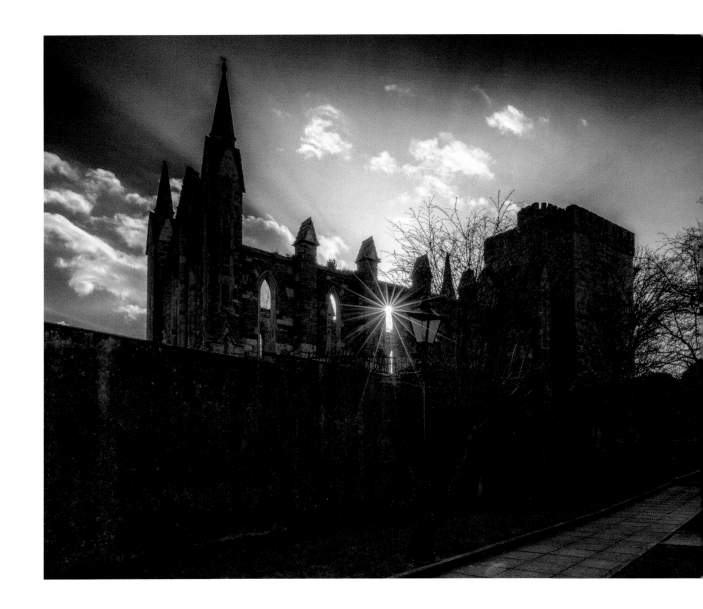

The Viking longships were of ingenious design. The up to 20 metre-long vessels were built to withstand the rough northern seas, but also designed to negotiate shallow rivers. Around 830 AD the small raiding parties of Norsemen were replaced by vast assault fleets. Forces of fifty ships or more not only attacked coastal settlements, but also went upstream right into the heart of Ireland and sacked the great monasteries such as Clonmacnoise and Clonfert.

At the time Ireland was divided into a number of small kingdoms whose rulers were too busy fighting each other to deal with this new threat from the outside. Within a few years of their first large-scale attacks the Vikings

begun to build permanent bases at the river estuaries of the east and south. These fortified harbours called 'Longphorts' would over time grow into centres of trade and commerce and evolve into Ireland's biggest towns and cities.

The Vikings, however, never attempted to bring the whole of Ireland under their control. Content in their own towns they mingled with the local population and left a lasting mark on Irish history. Many place names are of Old Norse origins and indicate where the Vikings built their settlements: Wexford 'Fjord of Veig', Wicklow 'Viking Meadow' or Waterford 'Windy Fjord'. Indeed 'Ireland' is the name given to the land of Erinn by the

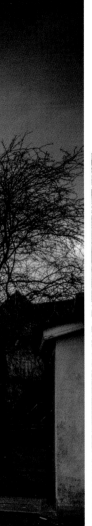

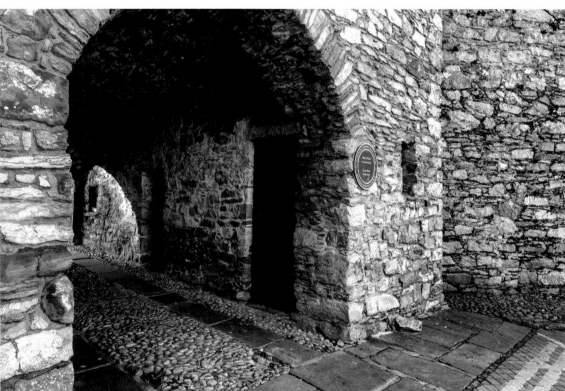

Left page: Selskar Abbey, Wexford Town
Right page: Westgate, Wexford Town

Vikings. Many of the common words we use today like 'market', 'anchor', 'helmet', 'boat' and many others are of Viking origin.

As the Viking towns and their wealth grew they became targets for the neighbouring Irish kingdoms; Dublin and Limerick were attacked and looted more than once.

Towards the end of the 10th century the power of the Vikings in Ireland begun to wane. There was no more support from the Scandinavian homeland and the Irish rulers increasingly sought to bring the Viking towns under their control. In 1014 a united Irish army under the command of Brian Boru, the first High King of the whole of Ireland, defeated the Vikings at the Battle of Clontarf, which is often marked as the end of the Viking era in Ireland.

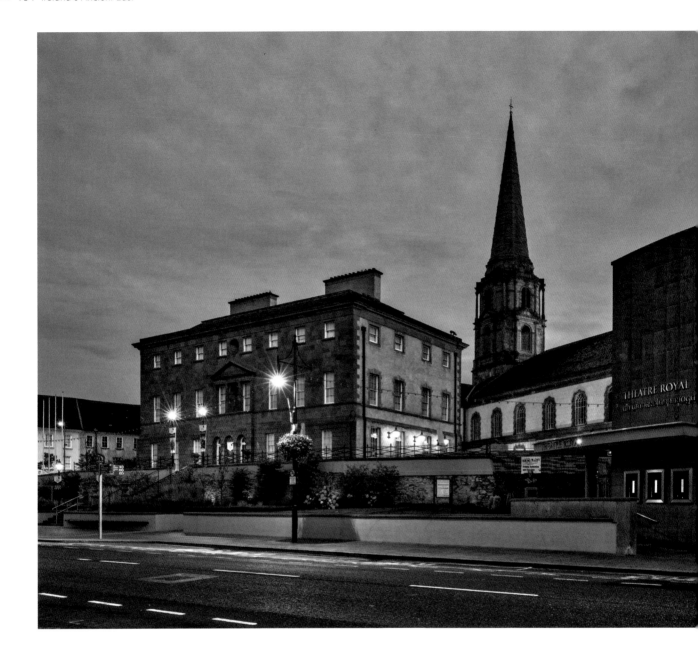

Waterford, standing on the shores of the River Suir about 27 kilometres away from where the river enters the sea, is Ireland's oldest city. There are a number of references to early Viking encampments in the area dating from 860 to 892 AD. The most popular story tells us about a Viking chieftain named Sitric Silkbeard who is said to have founded Waterford in 853 AD. Another version claims that the Norwegian king Harald Finehair (sometimes also called Fairhair) founded both Dublin and Waterford and later gave Waterford to his brother. Today the official foundation of Waterford as a permanent settlement is dated to 914 AD.

Reginald's Tower is the oldest civic building in Ireland. The tower formed the apex of the original Viking town and was re-built by the Anglo Normans in the 12th century when it became part of the medieval walls of the city.

In 1170, Waterford was taken by Anglo Norman forces under the command of Richard de Clare, better known as Strongbow, and allied Irish forces led by Dermot MacMurrough, King of Leinster. Wexford, the second major Viking town of the south east, had suffered the same fate the previous year.

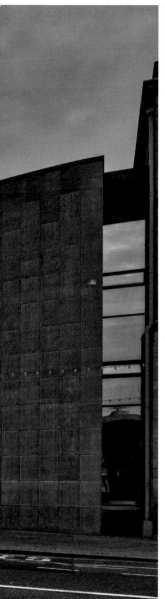

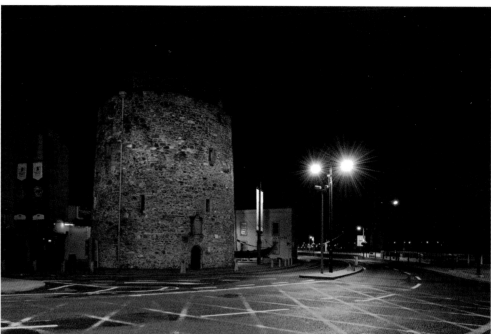

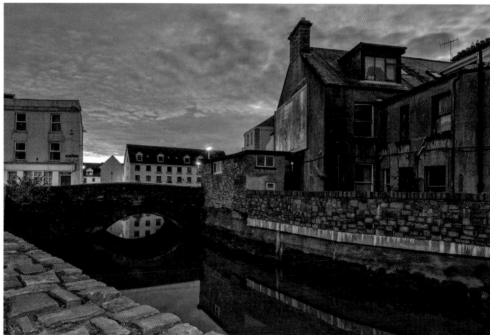

Left page: Bishop's Palace and Christchurch Cathedral, Waterford City
Right page top: Reginald's Tower, Waterford City
Right page bottom: John's River, Waterford City

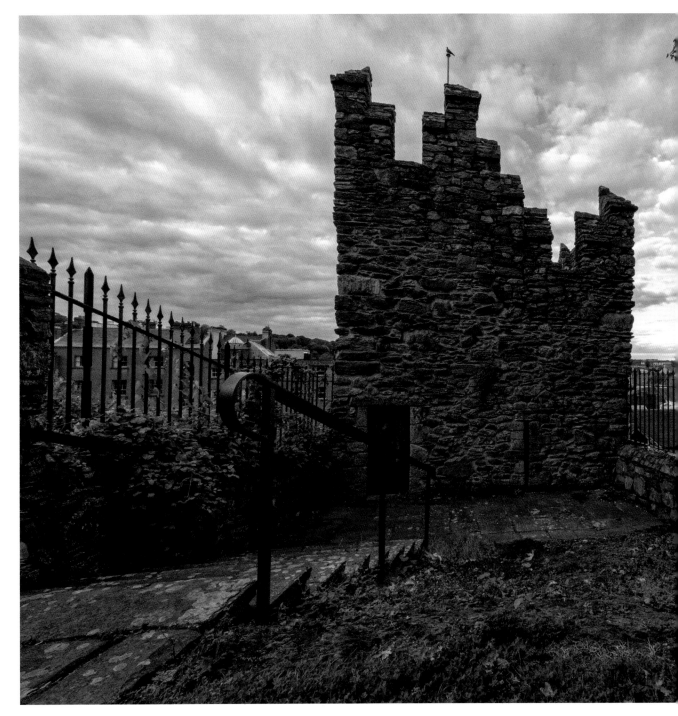

Left page: Beach Tower, Waterford City
Right page top: Old and new, Waterford City
Right page center: Chorister's Hall, Waterford City
Right page bottom: Door of St Olaf's hall, Waterford City

In 1171 Waterford was declared a royal city by King Henry II of England. Throughout the medieval period Waterford was Ireland's second city after Dublin and one of the most prosperous places in the country.

Today Waterford showcases a unique mixture of old and new: The ancient city walls stand beside modern office buildings. The 13th century Chorister's Hall and the 15th century Mayor's Wine Vault are now part of the purpose built Medieval Museum which stands right beside the 18th century Bishop's Palace which also acts as a museum. Just down the road stands Reginald's Tower (the third of Waterford's museums) opposite the steel and glass structure of a 20th century hotel.

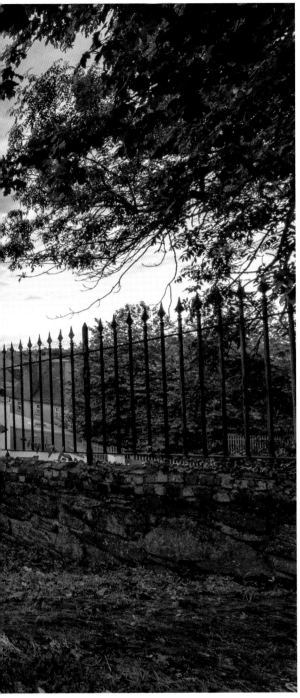

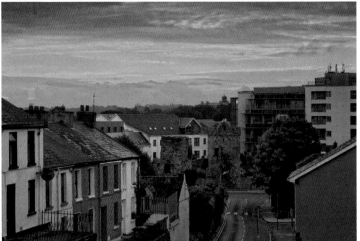

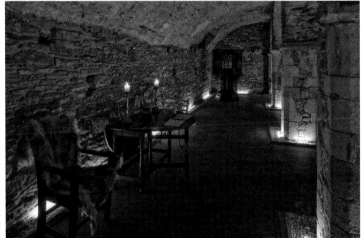

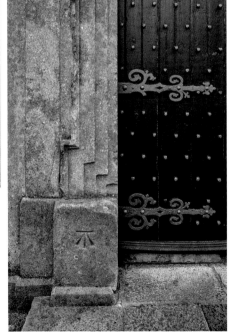

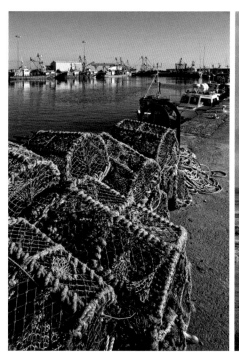
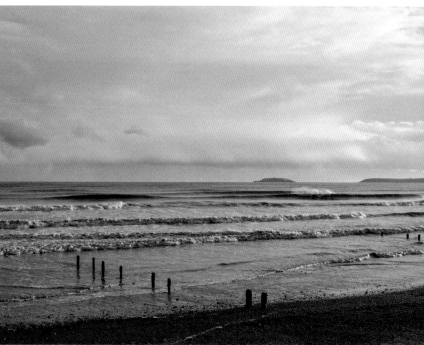

Left page top left: Kilmore Quay Harbour, County Wexford
Left page top right: Youghal Strand, Co. Cork
Right page: Cobh, Co. Cork

MARITIME GATEWAY

Youghal, from the Irish for 'Yew Wood', is a typical Irish seaside resort town at the estuary of the River Blackwater. Quiet in winter and bustling in summer. Its origins are strongly connected to the Vikings who had a settlement here from the 9th century. This settlement however wasn't permanent and under constant threat from neighbouring Irish clans. After the Norman invasion however the Irish and Vikings joined forces. The Normans had set out from their bases in Waterford and Wexford and met the united Irish and Viking warriors at the Mouth of the River Blackwater. The battle was fought on land and sea, but the better trained and equipped Normans had no real problem claiming victory. In 1177 Youghal was granted to Robert Fitzstephen and under his rule Youghal was transformed into a town. By the 14th century Youghal had become a major port and trading hub with connections to towns and cities all over Europe.

Sir Walter Raleigh, born around 1552 in Devon, was a colourful character, resided in Youghal and also was mayor of the town for a short period of time in 1588 and 1589. He had been granted a vast amount of land around Youghal and Lismore by Queen Elizabeth after being part of the suppression of the Desmond Rebellion in 1579. During his short residence at Myrtle Grove in Youghal he left a lasting impression. It is said that Raleigh planted the first potatoes in Ireland at Youghal and by doing so had a major impact on Irish history. Another story tells us about Sir Raleigh having a smoke in his garden. A servant, who had never seen tobacco before, thought Raleigh was on fire and to save his master threw a bucket of water over him.

Youghal weathered history and kept its status as one of the important ports in Ireland; it was one of only a few ports where wine could be discharged. In early 1600 Youghal became 'Staple Town' receiving the exclusive rights for trading wool with England; in 1603 the town was the chosen port for a royal visit when King James I was proclaimed on the quay in Youghal. In many 17th century texts the nearby Cork Harbour has been described as 'a port near Youghal', which says it all. Youghal even survived the Cromwellian invasion of 1649 relatively unscathed despite the fact that Cromwell made Youghal his winter quarters.

Only during the Great Famine Youghal begun to suffer with the rest of the country and despite recovering for a while its days as a major port were numbered. As the ships grew bigger they weren't able to enter the shallow estuary anymore and took their business to Cork and other deep-water ports.

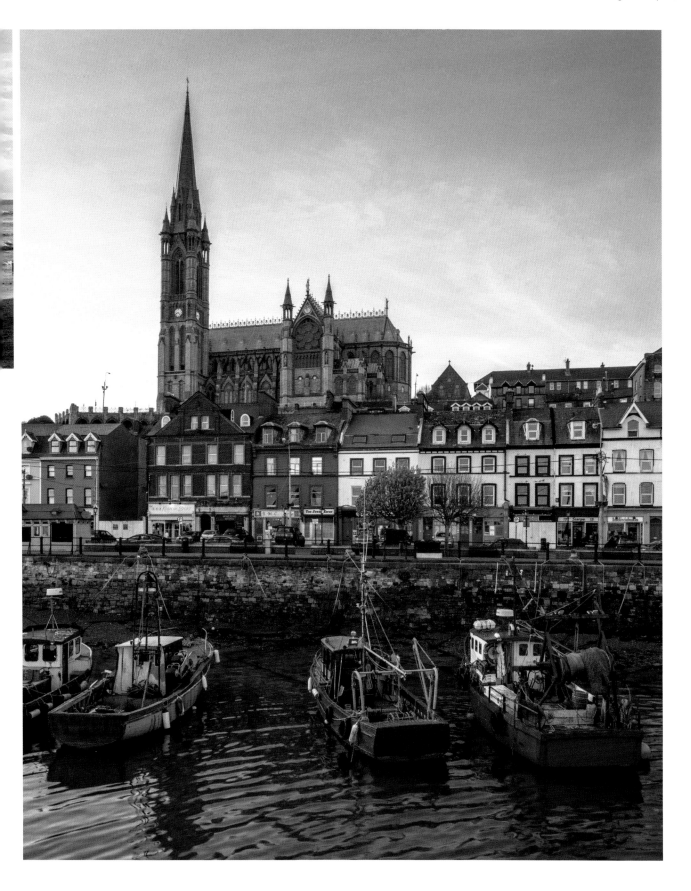

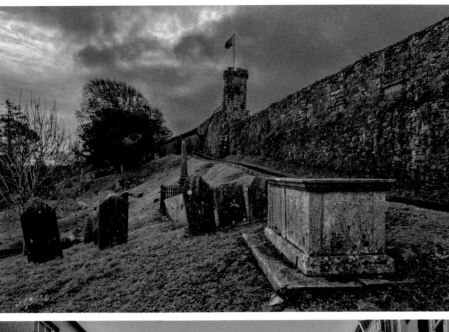

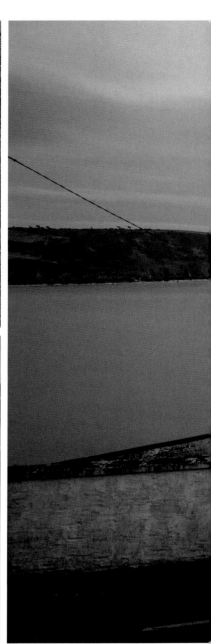

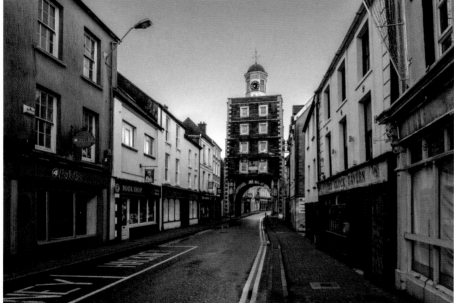

The first lighthouse at Youghal was built in 1202 together with a nunnery know as Chapel of St Anne's. The nuns maintained the light until around 1542. The current lighthouse was built between 1848 and 1852.

The Clock Gate Tower was built in 1777 and served as a prison during the 1798 rebellion. A number of rebel suspects were hanged from the lower windows of the tower while inside the tower suspects were tortured in various ways. One story tells us of Father Peter O'Neill who was flogged with 275 strikes to induce him to reveal the names of people involved in the rebellion heard in the confessional.

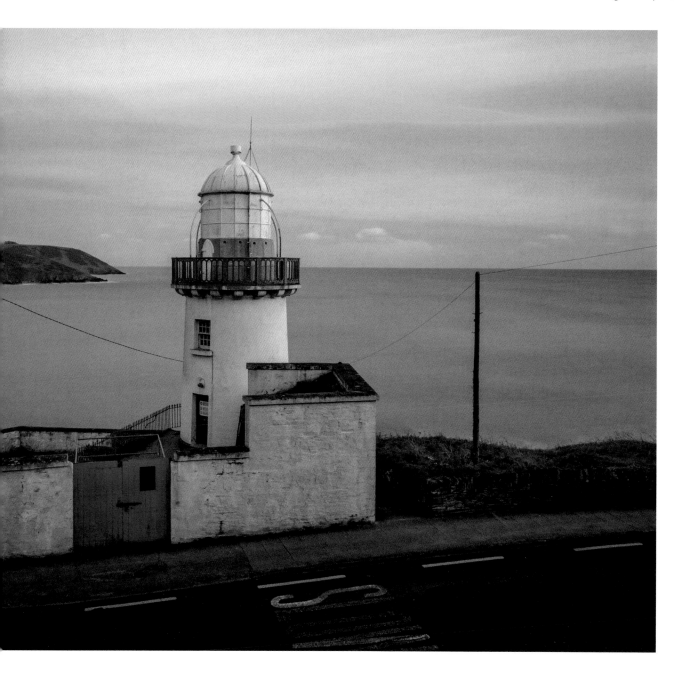

Left page top: Town Walls, Youghal, Co. Cork
Left page bottom: Youghal Clock Gate Tower, Co. Cork
Right page: Youghal Lighthouse, Co. Cork

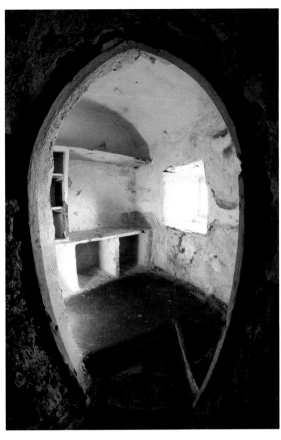
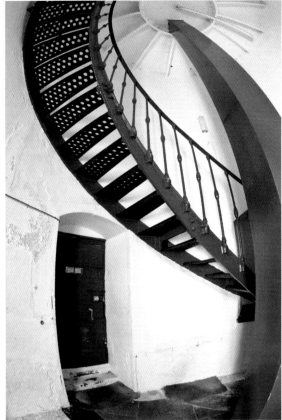
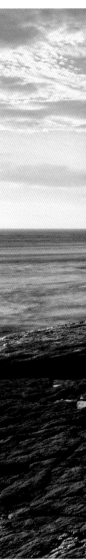
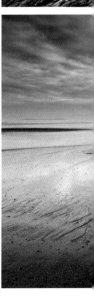

Left page: Hook Lighthouse, Co. Wexford
Right page top: Hook Lighthouse, Co. Wexford
Right page bottom left: Cullenstown Strand, County Wexford
Right page bottom right: Grange Strand, Hook Peninsula, Co. Wexford

The origins of Hook Lighthouse date back to early Christian times when St Dubhán founded a monastery on the peninsula which became known as 'Rinn Dubháin', Dubhan's Headland. According to legend the monks kept a signal fire going to keep approaching ships away from the treacherous rocks.

The Tower of Hook was built between 1210 and 1230 by William Marshall which makes it one of the oldest lighthouses in the world. The tower stands four stories and 35 metres high with walls up to four metres thick. The monks were kept on as lighthouse keepers and kept the fire going for several centuries. Numerous ghost stories surround the building, some telling of a monk still guarding the fire, others claim that William Marshall himself keeping vigil.

In 1791 the coal fire was replaced by a lamp burning whale oil which was subsequently replaced in 1871 by gas lights. In 1972 Hook Lighthouse became electric and in 1996 automated; the last lighthouse keeper left the Hook after some 800 years of almost uninterrupted service.

In 2001 the lighthouse was opened to the public and also hosts a visitor centre, coffee shop and bakery.

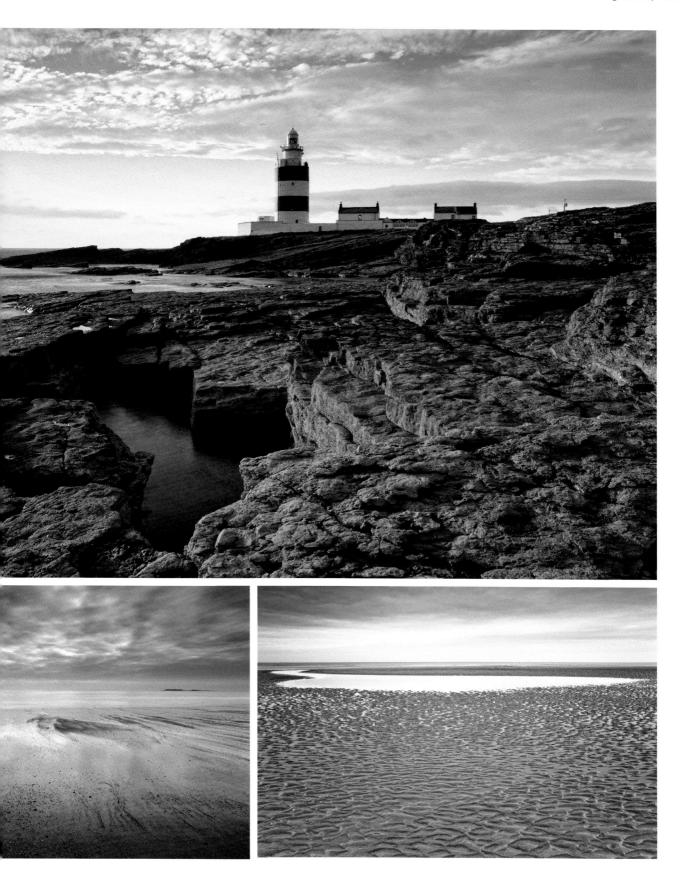

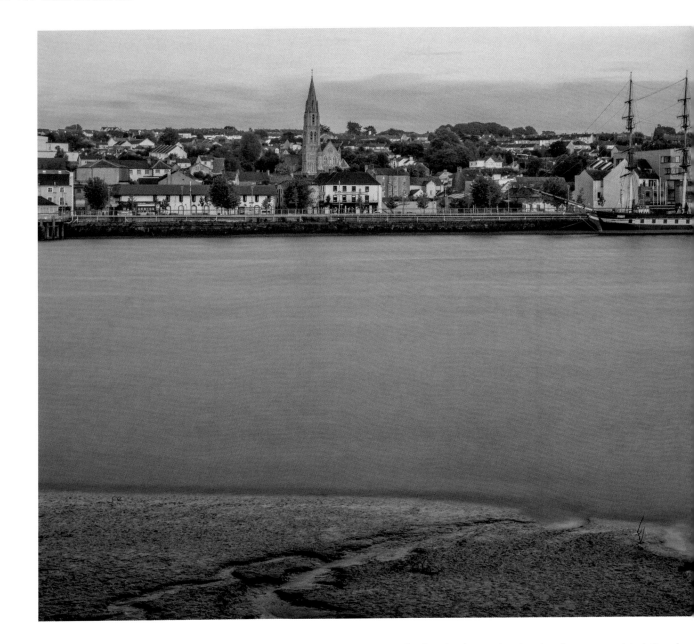

The Great Famine, *An Gorta Mór*, is one of the darkest chapters in Irish history. Although it wasn't the only famine in Ireland it has left the biggest mark on the country because its catastrophic results could have been prevented. Between 1845 and 1852 Ireland was struck by potato blight – a fungal infection of the potato plant. At the time more than one third of the Irish population was dependant on the potato as their main food source.

It would be impossible adequately to describe the privations which they [the Irish labourer and his family] habitually and silently endure ... in many districts their only food is the potato, their only beverage water ... their cabins are seldom a protection against the weather ... a bed or a blanket is a rare luxury ... and nearly in all their pig and a manure heap constitute their only property.

Earl of Devon, 1845

Many families already existed on the edge of starvation and the failing of the potato crop over several consecutive years had terrible consequences. During the Great Famine around one million people died, another million emigrated in what became known as 'coffin ships'.

The original *Dunbrody* was built as a cargo vessel in 1845 in Quebec. After the famine struck Ireland in the same year the owners of the *Dunbrody*, like many other ship owners, took advantage of the situation and fitted their vessel with bunks. Between 1845 and 1851 the *Dunbrody* carried thousands of emigrants to North America. Living space, food and water on board the Coffin Ships were scarce and as a consequence one third of the passengers didn't survive the journey. It is said that sharks were seen following the ships because so many dead bodies were thrown overboard.

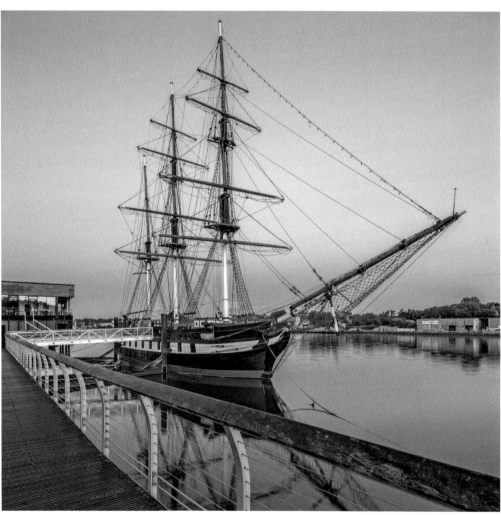

Left page: New Ross Dusk, Co. Wexford
Right page: Dunbrody Famine Ship, New Ross, Co. Wexford

The *Dunbrody* was detained in quarantine for five days because there were too many ships queuing in the St Lawrence River. Doctor Douglas is nearly single-handed ... every day, dozens of corpses are thrown overboard from many ships ... I have heard that some of them have no fresh water left and the passengers and crew have to drink the water from the river. God help them!

Captain Baldwin of the *Dunbrody* in a letter to William Graves, owner of the Dunbrody

The original *Dunbrody* ran aground in 1875 off the coast of Labrador with a cargo of timber and was damaged beyond repair. Today a replica 3-masted barque is docked near New Ross and can be visited to give a sense of life onboard a 'coffin ship'.

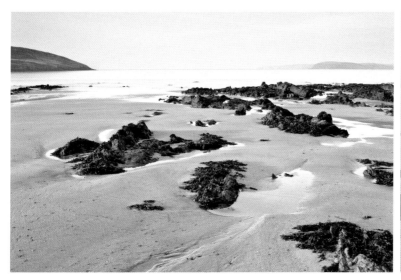
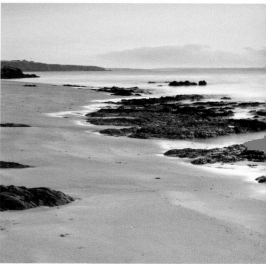

Left page left: Booley Bay, Hook Peninsula, Co. Wexford
Left page right: Baginbun Bay, Hook Peninsula, Co. Wexford
Right page: Ferns Castle, Co. Wexford

CASTLES AND CONQUESTS

Ferns was once the seat of the High King of Leinster Dermot Mac Murrough who will always be remembered as the man who brought the English to Ireland.

Dermot succeeded to the throne of Leinster in 1126 and soon earned a reputation as a ruthless leader with an eye on the high kingship of Ireland.

Dermot's biggest rival was Tiernan O'Rourke, King of Breifne, and an ongoing dispute about a stretch of fertile farm lands, escalated when Dermot abducted Tiernan's wife Dervorgilla and kept her at the castle at Ferns for a number of years. Some sources claim that Dervorgilla was glad to get away from her husband and that she was quite happy in her new surroundings.

Tiernan understandably was anything but happy and nurtured his grudge for a number of years. Some fifteen years after the abduction Tiernan managed to get the support of the Dublin Vikings and the King of Meath and together the marched on Leinster. The united armies devastated Dermot's kingdom and left the King of Leinster no other choice but to flee the country.

This was a turning point in Irish history. Dermot wasn't willing to accept his fate and in order to claim back his kingdom he approached King Henry II of England for help.

King Henry II granted his support to Dermot and allowed him to recruit an army. This culminated in August 1170, when an army under Richard de Clare (Strongbow) sailed over from England and took Waterford City. Strongbow married Dermot's daughter, Aoife, and Dermot recaptured his kingdom, but also laid the foundation to centuries of English rule and suppression.

Hear, noble king Henry,
Whence I was born, of what country.
Of Ireland I was born a lord, in Ireland acknowledged king;
But wrongfully my own people have cast me out of my kingdom.
To you I come to make plaint, good sire,
In the presence of the barons of your empire.
Your liege-man I shall become, henceforth all the days of my life,
On condition that you be my helper, so that I do not lose at all.
You I shall acknowledge as sire and lord, in the presence of your barons and earls.

Song of Dermot and the Earl

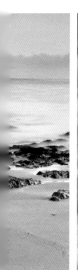

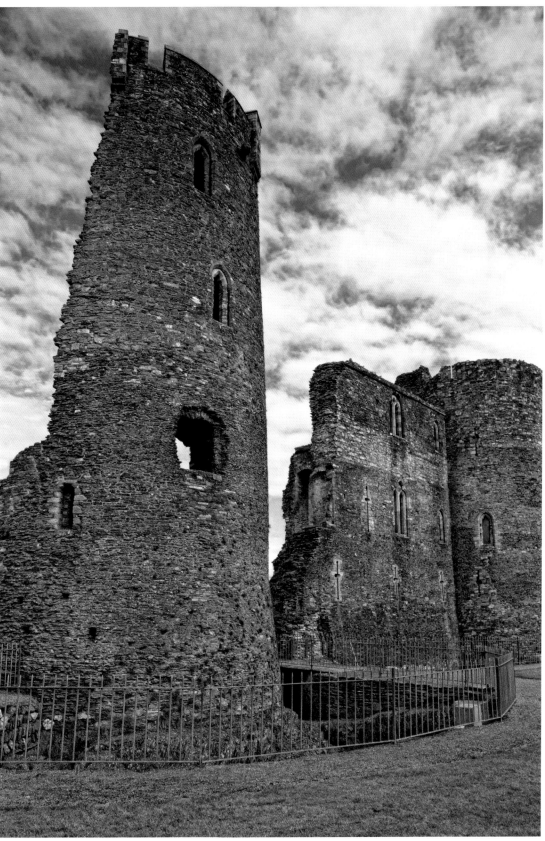

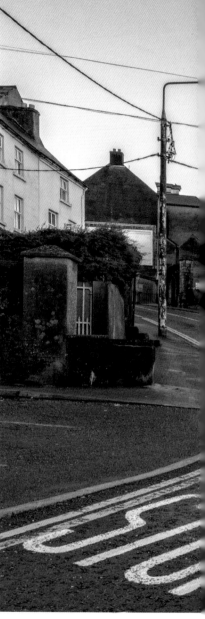

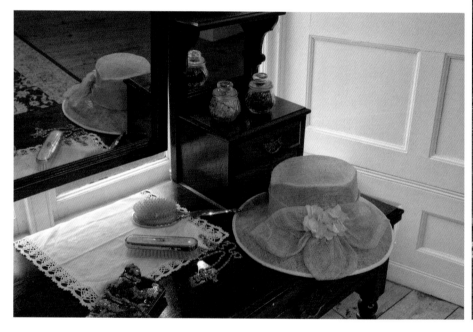

Enniscorthy Castle overlooks the river Slaney and today is in the centre of the town of the same name. The castle was built by Phillip de Prendergast and Maud de Quency a few decades after the first Norman invasion. Over the centuries it changed owners a number of times, not always peacefully.

In 1798 Enniscorthy and its castle took centre-stage as the final battleground of the United Irishmen Rebellion. What became known as The Battle of Vinegar Hill took place on the pudding-shaped hill overlooking Enniscorthy and along the streets of the town. The United Irishmen Rebellion broke out in May 1798 and quickly spread. The rebels had some initial success, especially in County Wexford but the English soon gained the upper hand. On June 18th some 20,000 English troops surrounded

Wexford with the goal of ending the rebellion in a single deadly strike. The rebel leaders gathered on Vinegar Hill in a last attempt to beat the English in one decisive battle. The two armies were almost equal in numbers, but the rebels were lacking firearms and experience.

The battle began at dawn with a massive artillery bombardment of the rebel positions on the hill. English troops moved in soon after supported by the relentless artillery fire. The Irish rebels were surrounded and pushed back. At the same time the English launched an attack on the town of Enniscorthy.

The rebels didn't stand much chance against the English firepower and their fight soon became desperate. Hundreds of rebels, as well as women

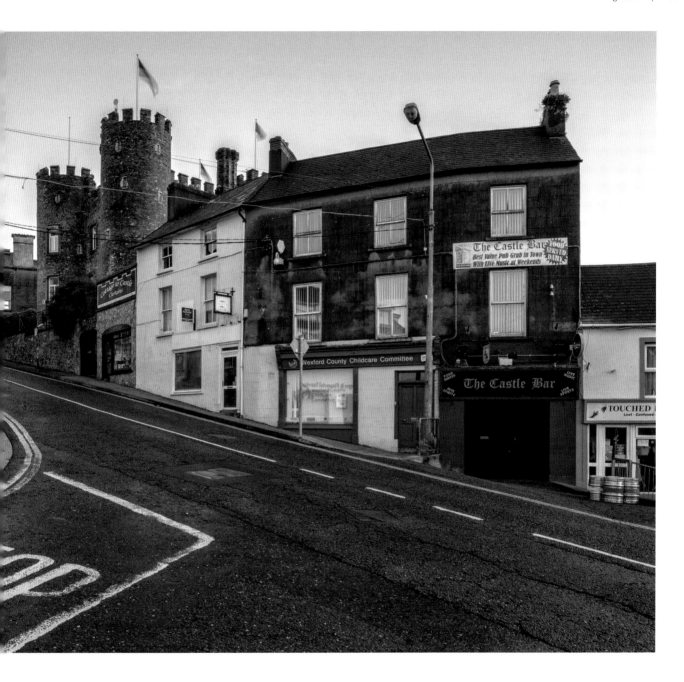

and children were killed. A small number of rebel forces however managed to escape through gaps in the English lines and teamed up with other rebel splinter groups. The organised rebellion had failed, but the Irish rebels kept resisting the English rule with raids and other guerrilla type operations.

Left page: Dressing Table, Enniscorthy Castle, Co. Wexford
Right page: Enniscorthy and Castle, Co. Wexford

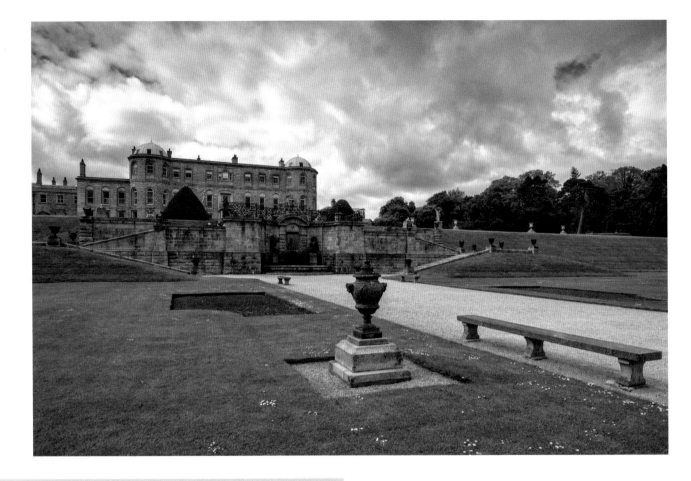

BIG HOUSES AND HARD TIMES

Powerscourt, set at the foothills of the Wicklow Mountains, is one of Ireland's greatest and best-known estates. Its story begins in 1609 when King James I. granted these lands to Sir Richard Wingfield, an army officer and adventurer from Sussex who was involved in both the Nine Year's War in Armagh and the Battle of Kinsale. The original grant stated:

'the manor of Powerscourt, containing one ruinous castle … and all lands in the whole country of Fercullen conteininge in itself 5 miles in leinth and 4 in bredth, for the most part mountaine and stonie … to hold for 21 years at a rent of £6 Ierishe'.

The name 'Powerscourt' probably derives from the earlier owners, the LePoer family who came to Ireland in the 12th century during the Strongbow invasion: 'LePoer' became' Power' and the added 'court' suggest that a castle had existed on the site for quite a while.

In 1618 Richard was elevated to Viscount Powerscourt, which cost him a fee of 2,000 pounds; Richard and his wife Frances Cromwell had no children and the title expired with Richard's death in 1635.

The lands and wealth fell to Richard's cousin Sir Edward Wingfield of Carnew, who in turn was succeeded by his son Richard; this Richard faced a tumultuous era of rebellion in Ireland, civil war in England and the rise of Oliver Cromwell. During this time Powerscourt was burned out by Irish forces.

Powerscourt then fell to Richard's son, Folliot Wingfield, who restored the estate and eventually was granted the title Viscount Powerscourt in

1665. It was during Folliot's time that the Powerscourt as it is today and the nearby village of Enniskerry began to develop.

Folliot and his wife passed away without an heir and the estate fell to his cousin Edward Wingfield in 1717 who passed it on to his son Richard. Richard, who also was granted the title Viscount Powerscourt, transformed the medieval castle that had been the family seat at Powerscourt into the grand mansion we can see today.

Over the following generations the Viscounts Powerscourt built and developed both the mansion and gardens. In 1961 the Slazenger family purchased the estate from the 9th Viscount Powerscourt. The new owners started a major refurbishment of the house and gardens in order to make it a visitor attraction when in the early hours of 4 November 1974 disaster struck: a fire broke out on the top floor and quickly spread throughout the house. By midmorning the grand building was nothing but a roofless shell.

Over twenty years later, in 1996, Powerscourt eventually opened its doors to the public. Today the house, garden and wider landscape are one of Ireland's major tourist attractions and feature a few superlatives: Powerscourt Waterfall is the highest in Ireland, the pet cemetery, with its very personal and intimate headstones, is the largest in Europe and the view from the Italian Garden over Triton's Lake to Sugar Loaf Mountain in the distance is one that is not easily forgotten.

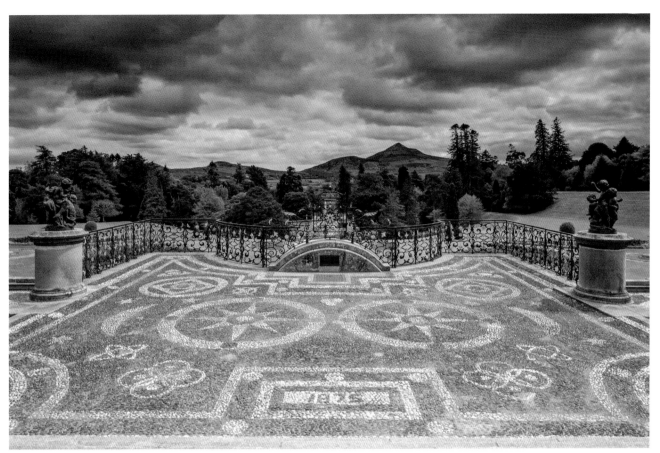

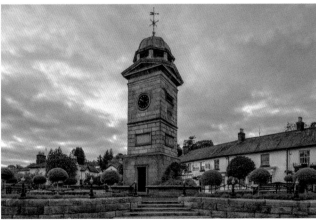

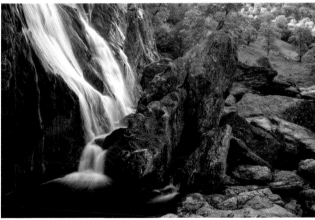

Left page: Powerscourt House, Co. Wicklow
Right page top: Powerscourt, Co. Wicklow
Right page bottom left: Enniskerry, Co. Wicklow
Right page bottom right: Powerscourt Waterfall, Co. Wicklow

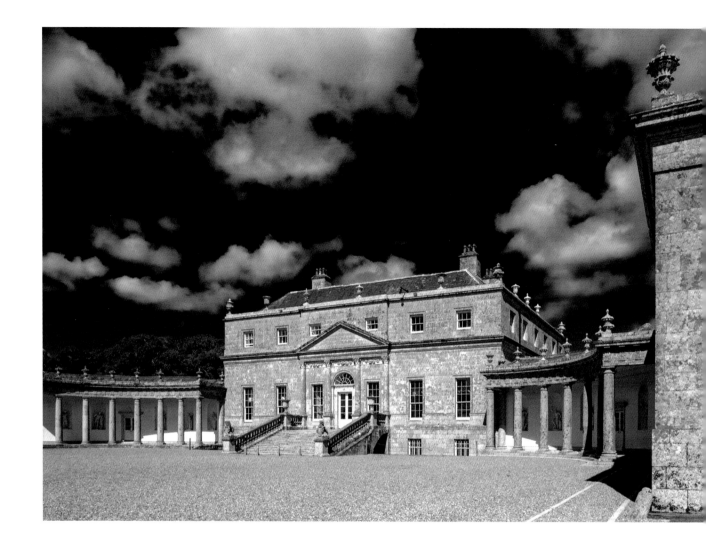

Russborough House is situated near the Blessington Lakes in County Wicklow and is one of the finest examples of Palladian architecture in the country. This style of architecture was derived and inspired by the designs of Venetian architect Andrea Palladio who in turn based his designs on the classical architecture of the ancient Greek and Roman temples. It's also reputedly the longest house in Ireland with a frontage measuring 210 metres.

Russborough House was built between 1741 and 1750 for Joseph Leeson, whose family came originally from Northamptonshire in England, but settled in Ireland in the second half of the 17th century where they made a fortune in brewing and property development. Joseph Leeson went into politics, became an MP and received the title of Earl of Milltown in 1763. The title and the house were then passed on from father to son for six generations. When the 6th Earl of Milltown passed away without an heir the house went to a nephew, Sir Edmund Turton. After his death Russborough House changed owners a couple of times until in 1952 when Sir Alfred and Lady Beit bought the estate to be their home and house their art collection.

In 1976 the childless couple established the Alfred Beit Foundation to preserve Russborough and make it accessible to the public and in 1978 Russborough opened its doors for the first time. Sir Alfred passed away in 1994 and his wife Clementine lived on at Russborough until her death in 2005.

Today the Russborough Estate is still managed by the Alfred Beit Foundation and the house and grounds are still open to visitors.

Beside the artworks and architecture Russborough also houses a number of traditional artisans including wood turners, blacksmiths and stone masons and offers parkland walks and a coffee shop with local produce.